HOW TO START A MEDICAL MARIJUANA BUSINESS

Stay Relevant While Overcoming Challenges, Seizing Opportunities and following Regulations in the Cannabis industry

Jeanelle K. Douglas

Copyright © 2024 by Jeanelle K. Douglas. All rights reserved.

DEDICATION

To the reader who holds this book. You hold the key to unlocking this journey.

Thank you for joining me.

Contents

Introduction 8
   Overview of the Medical Marijuana Industry 8
   Benefits of Opening a Medical Marijuana Dispensary 11

Understanding Legal Frameworks 14
   Federal vs. State Laws 17
   Key legal considerations and compliance 20

Licensing Requirements and Application Process 24
   Pre-application requirements 27
   Submitting Your Application 30
   Post-Application Steps 34

Market Research and Business Planning 38
   Analyzing the Market Demand for Medical Marijuana 41
   Identifying Your Target Market 44
   Competitive Analysis 47
   Crafting a Detailed Business Plan 50
   Executive Summary 53
   Company Description 56
   Market Analysis 59
   Organization and Management 62

- Sales Strategies 65
- Funding Request 68
- Financial Projections 71
- Financial Planning and Management 75
  - Estimating Start-Up Costs 78
  - Understanding the Sources of Funding 82
  - Budgeting and Financial Management 85
  - Banking and Financial Services for Marijuana Businesses 89
  - Challenges Faced by Marijuana Businesses 90
  - Emerging Solutions and Alternatives 91
- Location Selection and Leasing 93
  - Considerations for Location Selection 93
  - Securing a Lease 95
  - Zoning and location criteria 97
  - Navigating Zoning and Location Criteria 100
  - Financial Terms 104
  - Designing Your Dispensary for Success 105
- Licensing and Compliance 109
  - Compliance Considerations 111
  - Navigating the Licensing Process 113

Compliance with State and Local Regulations........................ 118

Record-Keeping and Reporting Requirements........................ 121

Product Acquisition and Inventory Management........................ 125

Product Acquisition 125

Inventory Management 126

Establishing Relationships with Growers and Suppliers.......... 128

Building Relationships 130

Cultivating a Network 132

Choosing product assortments 132

Inventory Management Practices 136

Staffing Your Dispensary.. 140

Hiring Qualified Staff.. 144

Training and Education for Employees................................... 147

Staff Management and Retention Strategies 150

Security Measures 154

Physical security requirements.. 157

Security Protocols and Procedures 161

Compliance with Security Regulations 165

Marketing and Customer Relations... 169

Building a brand for your dispensary...................................... 173

Marketing Strategies and Channels 177
Customer Service and Retention Strategies 180
Operational Management 184
Daily Operations and Workflow 188
Quality Control and Product Safety 192
Handling Customer Feedback and Complaints 195
Ethical Considerations and Community Engagement 199
Social Responsibility in The Cannabis Industry 202
Engaging with the community 205
Environmental Considerations 209
Scaling and Expansion 212
Evaluating the Performance Of Your Dispensary 216
Opportunities for Scaling and Expansion 219
Strategies for Growth and Diversification 222
Legal and Industry Updates 227
Why Staying Updated is Critical 227
Staying informed about legal changes 231
Keeping Up With Industry Trends 235
Conclusion 239

Introduction

Overview of the Medical Marijuana Industry

The medical marijuana industry, a burgeoning sector within the broader cannabis market, has witnessed a remarkable trajectory of growth and transformation in recent decades. This evolution is underpinned by a significant shift in societal attitudes, legal frameworks, and scientific understanding of cannabis's therapeutic potential. At its core, the industry aims to harness the medicinal properties of marijuana to improve the quality of life for patients with a variety of conditions and symptoms.

Initially marginalized and enveloped in legal and social controversy, medical marijuana has gradually emerged as a legitimate area of interest for medical research and a viable option for patients seeking alternative treatments. This shift has been catalyzed by a growing body of scientific research that underscores the potential benefits of cannabis in treating a wide array of medical conditions, including but not limited to chronic pain, epilepsy, multiple sclerosis, and the side effects of chemotherapy.

These findings have played a crucial role in reshaping public opinion and influencing policy decisions, leading to the legalization of medical marijuana in numerous jurisdictions around the world.

The legal landscape of the medical marijuana industry is complex and varies significantly across different regions. In some areas, comprehensive regulatory frameworks have been established to govern the cultivation, distribution, and sale of medical marijuana, ensuring patient access while addressing concerns related to safety, quality control, and misuse prevention.

However, in other regions, medical marijuana remains entangled in legal restrictions, reflecting ongoing debates over its classification, potential risks, and therapeutic efficacy.

Economically, the industry has become a significant driver of growth, generating substantial revenue, creating jobs, and attracting investment. From cultivation and processing to dispensaries and ancillary services, the medical marijuana supply chain encompasses a diverse array of businesses and professionals, including growers, researchers, healthcare providers, and entrepreneurs. This economic activity not only contributes to local and national economies but also spurs innovation in product development, delivery methods, and patient care.

Despite its progress and potential, the medical marijuana industry faces several challenges and controversies. Regulatory hurdles, banking restrictions, and the need for more clinical research are among the key issues that stakeholders continue to navigate.

Additionally, concerns about product consistency, access disparities, and social equity highlight the need for ongoing efforts to address these challenges responsibly and ethically.

Looking ahead, the future of the medical marijuana industry is poised for further expansion and evolution. As legal barriers continue to diminish and societal acceptance grows, the industry is expected to play an increasingly prominent role in healthcare and wellness. Continued research and technological advancements will likely unlock new therapeutic applications and improve patient experiences. However, achieving sustainable growth and maximizing the therapeutic potential of medical marijuana will require a balanced approach that considers the interests and concerns of all stakeholders involved.

The medical marijuana industry stands at a crossroads of opportunity and challenge, reflecting broader societal shifts toward a more nuanced understanding of cannabis and its place in the medical field. Its journey from the fringes to the forefront of medical research and treatment highlights the dynamic interplay between science, policy, and public perception, underscoring the complex but promising path forward for medical marijuana.

Benefits of Opening a Medical Marijuana Dispensary

Opening a medical marijuana dispensary offers a unique set of benefits that extend beyond the individual business owner to the patients it serves and the community at large. At its heart, this venture taps into the growing acceptance and legal recognition of cannabis for therapeutic purposes, positioning dispensaries as key players in a transformative health and wellness industry.

One of the primary advantages of opening a medical marijuana dispensary is the opportunity to contribute positively to patient health and wellbeing. Dispensaries provide patients with legal, safe, and regulated access to medical cannabis, which can be a crucial component of treatment for a variety of conditions.

For many patients, traditional medications may not be effective, may cause undesirable side effects, or may even lead to dependency issues. Medical marijuana offers an alternative or complementary option that, for some, has proven to be more effective in managing their symptoms.

By operating a dispensary, owners play a direct role in improving the quality of life for these individuals, offering not just products but support, education, and a sense of community.

Financially, dispensaries represent a lucrative business opportunity in an industry that has seen exponential growth over the past decade. With increasing legalization and a shift in public perception, the demand for medical cannabis continues to rise. This growth translates into robust revenue potential for dispensaries, which, when managed effectively, can yield significant profits.

The economic benefits also extend to job creation, contributing to local employment opportunities in various roles, including retail, cultivation, and management. Dispensaries can contribute to the normalization and de-stigmatization of cannabis use for medical purposes. By operating professional, transparent, and community-focused establishments, dispensary owners can help shift public opinion and foster a more informed and open dialogue about cannabis and its place in healthcare. This cultural shift is critical for advancing cannabis research, improving access, and refining regulations to better serve patients and communities.

Opening a dispensary also offers an entrepreneurial avenue to participate in an emerging market with room for innovation. The cannabis industry is rapidly evolving, and dispensaries are at the forefront of developing new products, delivery methods, and patient services. This dynamic environment encourages creativity and adaptability, allowing dispensary owners to differentiate their offerings and cater to the specific needs of their patient base.

From specialized strains and formulations to educational programs and wellness services, dispensaries have the potential to shape the future of medical cannabis.

Operating a medical marijuana dispensary comes with the potential for significant community impact. Beyond providing access to treatment, dispensaries can engage in educational outreach, advocate for patient rights, and support local initiatives. Many dispensaries invest in community relations by sponsoring events, participating in public health campaigns, and contributing to local charities. These activities not only strengthen the community but also build goodwill and support for the dispensary and the broader medical marijuana industry.

Opening a medical marijuana dispensary offers a multifaceted opportunity to make a positive impact on individual lives, contribute to the growth of a burgeoning industry, and engage with the community in meaningful ways. While challenges and responsibilities come with operating within this space, the benefits—ranging from financial rewards to the profound satisfaction of enhancing patient wellbeing—present a compelling case for those considering entering the medical marijuana market.

Understanding Legal Frameworks

Understanding the legal frameworks surrounding the medical marijuana industry is crucial for anyone looking to operate within this space. The landscape is characterized by a complex interplay of laws and regulations that vary significantly from one jurisdiction to another, reflecting a diverse range of policies, attitudes, and historical contexts.

This complexity is further compounded by the evolving nature of cannabis legislation, as governments continue to grapple with issues related to medical use, recreational use, and hemp cultivation.

The legal frameworks governing medical marijuana is the distinction between federal and state (or local) laws in countries like the United States. Federally, marijuana remains classified as a controlled substance, which poses a range of challenges for businesses operating in states where medical cannabis has been legalized.

This dichotomy creates a legal gray area, affecting everything from banking and taxation to research and interstate commerce. Entrepreneurs must navigate these federal constraints while complying with state regulations that dictate how medical marijuana can be cultivated, distributed, and sold.

State laws themselves vary widely, with each jurisdiction establishing its own set of rules regarding licensing, product testing, packaging, and patient access. These regulations are designed to ensure product safety and quality, prevent diversion to the recreational market, and protect public health. Prospective dispensary owners must undergo a rigorous application process that typically involves demonstrating compliance with security, record-keeping, and operational standards. This process may also require applicants to show financial viability, community support, and plans for patient education and community engagement.

Local ordinances can introduce additional layers of regulation, including zoning laws that dictate where dispensaries can be located. These laws often aim to keep dispensaries away from schools, parks, and other sensitive areas, while also addressing community concerns about safety and property values. Navigating these local regulations is essential for securing a suitable location for a dispensary and for fostering positive relationships with the community.

Compliance is a continuous responsibility for dispensary operators, requiring ongoing attention to legal updates and regulatory changes. The dynamic nature of cannabis legislation means that laws and regulations can evolve rapidly, often in response to shifting public opinion, political landscapes, or emerging research. Staying informed and adaptable is key to maintaining compliance and ensuring the longevity of the business.

In addition to regulatory compliance, understanding legal frameworks also involves recognizing the potential for legal disputes and challenges. This might include issues related to intellectual property, employment law, or disputes with regulators. Dispensary operators must be prepared to navigate these challenges, often requiring legal counsel specialized in cannabis law.

Beyond the complexities and challenges, the legal frameworks governing medical marijuana also offer opportunities for advocacy and engagement. Many in the industry play an active role in shaping policy, advocating for reform, and working towards a more equitable and effective regulatory environment. This includes efforts to improve patient access, promote social equity, and support research into the medical uses of cannabis.

Understanding the legal frameworks of the medical marijuana industry is a multifaceted endeavor that requires diligence, expertise, and a proactive approach. It involves not only adhering to existing laws and regulations but also anticipating changes, engaging with the community and policymakers, and advocating for a legal environment that supports the safe, responsible, and beneficial use of medical cannabis.

Federal vs. State Laws

The interplay between federal and state laws is a defining characteristic of the legal landscape for medical marijuana in countries like the United States, creating a complex environment for businesses, patients, and regulators alike. This tension arises from the fundamental differences in how federal and state governments classify and regulate cannabis, leading to a patchwork of regulations that can be challenging to navigate.

At the federal level, marijuana is classified as a Schedule one controlled substance under the Controlled Substances Act (CSA). This classification is based on criteria such as a high potential for abuse, a lack of accepted medical use in the United States, and a lack of accepted safety for use under medical supervision.

As a result, federal law prohibits the cultivation, distribution, and possession of marijuana, with no exceptions for medical use. This stance impacts various aspects of the medical marijuana industry, from banking and taxation to research and interstate commerce. For example, businesses operating in compliance with state medical marijuana laws may still face risks of federal enforcement actions, and they often encounter significant barriers in accessing banking services or securing federal tax benefits due to the illicit status of marijuana under federal law.

Contrastingly, a growing number of states have enacted laws that allow for the medical use of cannabis, reflecting a shift in public opinion and an increasing recognition of cannabis's potential therapeutic benefits. These state laws vary widely but generally establish regulatory frameworks for the cultivation, distribution, and use of medical marijuana. They may define conditions for which medical marijuana can be recommended, establish systems for patient registration and identification cards, and set standards for businesses operating in the industry. State regulations also cover a range of operational aspects, including licensing requirements, product testing and labeling, and security measures.

The divergence between federal and state laws creates a legal gray area for individuals and businesses engaged in the medical marijuana industry. While state laws may protect them from state-level prosecution, they remain vulnerable to federal actions. This discrepancy has prompted calls for reform at the federal level, with proposals ranging from reclassifying marijuana under the CSA to enacting laws that would recognize and protect state-legal cannabis activities from federal interference.

The conflict between federal and state laws also has broader implications for policy, research, and healthcare. For instance, the federal prohibition of marijuana limits the scope of research into its medical applications, hindering the development of evidence-based policies and treatments. It also affects the ability of healthcare providers to discuss or recommend medical cannabis to their patients, impacting patient care and access to alternative therapies.

Efforts to resolve the tension between federal and state laws continue, with legislative proposals, court cases, and policy discussions seeking to address the complex issues raised by the current legal landscape. These efforts are informed by a growing body of research, changing public attitudes towards cannabis, and the experiences of states that have legalized medical marijuana.

As this legal and policy dialogue evolves, it may lead to significant changes in how medical marijuana is regulated and understood in the United States, potentially harmonizing federal and state laws in a way that supports patient access, promotes public health and safety, and acknowledges the therapeutic potential of cannabis.

Key legal considerations and compliance

Navigating the legal considerations and ensuring compliance are paramount for anyone operating or looking to establish a medical marijuana dispensary. The intricate web of regulations that govern the industry requires a thorough understanding and meticulous adherence to a range of legal requirements. This commitment to compliance not only protects the business from potential legal liabilities but also plays a crucial role in legitimizing and advancing the medical marijuana industry as a whole.

First and foremost, understanding the specific state and local laws where the dispensary operates is essential. These laws can dictate everything from where a dispensary can be located, based on zoning regulations, to how products must be stored, labeled, and sold. Each jurisdiction may have its unique set of rules regarding the documentation required for patient eligibility, the types of products that can be sold, and the advertising of cannabis products. Staying abreast of these laws and regulations, which can frequently change, is critical for maintaining compliance.

Licensing requirements form another crucial legal consideration for dispensaries. Most states with legal medical marijuana frameworks have established detailed application processes for obtaining a dispensary license. These processes often involve demonstrating financial stability, submitting detailed business plans, and passing background checks. In some cases, there may be a limited number of licenses available, making the application process highly competitive. Once obtained, maintaining that license requires ongoing compliance with state regulations, including regular reporting and adherence to operational standards.

Security measures are also a key legal requirement for medical marijuana dispensaries. States typically mandate specific security protocols to prevent theft and diversion of cannabis products. These measures can include surveillance systems, secure storage for cannabis products, and detailed tracking systems that account for the product from seed to sale. Ensuring that these security measures are in place and functioning correctly is vital for compliance and for the safety of the dispensary's employees and customers.

Another area of legal concern is the adherence to health and safety regulations. This includes ensuring that cannabis products are tested for potency and contaminants by licensed laboratories, as well as implementing protocols to ensure that products are handled, stored, and dispensed in a manner that maintains their quality and safety. Compliance in this area protects patients and underscores the dispensary's commitment to providing safe and reliable products.

Financial compliance is another complex aspect, particularly given the discrepancies between state and federal laws regarding cannabis. Many banks and financial institutions are federally insured and are hesitant to provide services to cannabis-related businesses due to the federal prohibition of marijuana. This situation forces many dispensaries to operate primarily in cash, which presents challenges for tax compliance, payroll, and general accounting practices. Dispensaries must navigate these challenges carefully, maintaining meticulous financial records and adhering to tax laws to remain in compliance.

Privacy laws regarding patient information are also paramount in the medical marijuana industry. Dispensaries must ensure that they are in compliance with state laws regarding the protection of patient records, which may involve securing written consent from patients before their information can be shared and implementing strict protocols for how patient information is stored and accessed.

Navigating the evolving landscape of medical marijuana laws requires a proactive approach to legal compliance. This includes staying informed about legislative changes, participating in industry associations, and seeking legal counsel when necessary. It also involves advocating for policies and regulations that support the needs of patients while ensuring the safe and responsible operation of dispensaries.

The Key legal considerations and compliance in the medical marijuana industry encompass a wide range of issues, from licensing and security to health and safety standards, financial practices, and patient privacy. Navigating these complexities requires diligence, expertise, and a commitment to operating within the bounds of the law, all of which are essential for the success and sustainability of a medical marijuana dispensary.

Licensing Requirements and Application Process

The process of obtaining a license to operate a medical marijuana dispensary is intricate and varies significantly from one jurisdiction to another, reflecting the unique legal and regulatory landscapes of different states or countries. Despite these variations, the licensing process generally involves several key steps designed to ensure that applicants meet the stringent requirements set forth by regulatory authorities. This process aims to safeguard public health and safety, ensure product quality, and prevent the diversion of cannabis to non-medical use.

The initial step in the licensing process typically requires applicants to demonstrate a clear understanding of the medical marijuana industry, including compliance with specific legal and operational guidelines. Applicants must often provide detailed business plans that outline their proposed operation, including information on the sourcing of products, security measures, and plans for patient education. These business plans also need to address financial projections and demonstrate the financial stability of the applicants, underscoring their ability to sustain operations over time.

One of the most critical aspects of the application process is the background check. Regulatory bodies conduct thorough background checks on all applicants and their key employees to ensure there are no criminal histories that could pose a risk to the program's integrity. This scrutiny extends to financial background checks to identify any potential financial liabilities that could impact the business's operational security.

Securing a suitable location for the dispensary is another vital component of the licensing process. Applicants must navigate local zoning laws and regulations, which often specify where dispensaries can be located, such as certain distances from schools, parks, and other dispensaries. The chosen location must also comply with security requirements and accessibility standards to ensure safe access for patients.

The application process often involves a non-refundable application fee, which can be substantial. This fee covers the cost of processing the application and the regulatory oversight required to evaluate the applicant's suitability. In competitive markets, where the number of licenses is limited, the process may also include a scoring system based on various criteria, such as the applicant's business plan, security measures, and contributions to community health and safety. This competitive aspect underscores the importance of thorough preparation and attention to detail in the application.

Once an application is submitted, the review process can be lengthy, involving multiple stages of assessment by the regulatory body. During this time, applicants may be required to provide additional information or clarification on their plans and proposals. Approval is not guaranteed, and applicants must often navigate a complex web of regulatory requirements and evaluations.

Upon receiving a license, the work is not over. Dispensary operators must adhere to ongoing compliance requirements, including regular inspections, renewals of the license, and continuous reporting on various aspects of their operations. Failure to maintain compliance can result in penalties, including the revocation of the license.

In addition to the primary dispensary license, there may be additional permits and approvals required, such as those related to building and safety codes, environmental regulations, and health department certifications. Each of these elements adds another layer of complexity to the licensing process, requiring applicants to navigate a multifaceted regulatory environment.

The licensing process for medical marijuana dispensaries, while daunting, is designed to ensure that only qualified and responsible operators are granted the privilege of serving medical marijuana patients. It reflects a commitment to the safe and effective use of cannabis for medical purposes, balancing the need for access with the imperative of protecting public health and safety.

As the medical marijuana industry continues to evolve, so too will the licensing processes and requirements, reflecting ongoing developments in legislation, regulation, and best practices.

Pre-application requirements

The pre-application requirements for opening a medical marijuana dispensary serve as a foundational step in the licensing process, ensuring that potential applicants are well-prepared and qualified to enter the complex and highly regulated medical marijuana industry. These requirements vary across jurisdictions but typically encompass a series of steps and criteria designed to ensure applicants have a solid understanding of the industry, the legal landscape, and the responsibilities involved in operating a dispensary.

One of the first steps in the pre-application phase often involves attending informational sessions or workshops hosted by the regulatory body overseeing medical marijuana in the jurisdiction. These sessions provide valuable insights into the regulatory environment, application process, and operational requirements, helping applicants to fully grasp the scope of what's involved in running a dispensary.

Conducting thorough research and due diligence is another critical aspect of the pre-application requirements. Applicants are expected to familiarize themselves with the specific laws, regulations, and guidelines that govern the medical marijuana industry in their jurisdiction. This research should cover everything from licensing and operational requirements to zoning laws and security protocols. Understanding these regulations is crucial for developing a compliant business plan and avoiding potential legal and operational pitfalls down the line.

Developing a detailed business plan is also a key component of the pre-application process. This plan should outline the applicant's proposed business model, including information on product sourcing, inventory management, patient education, security measures, and community engagement strategies. Financial projections, funding sources, and a detailed budget should also be included to demonstrate the financial viability of the dispensary. The business plan serves not only as a roadmap for the applicant but also as a critical document for the licensing application, showcasing the applicant's preparedness and understanding of the industry.

Securing the right location is another essential pre-application requirement. Applicants must identify a suitable site for their dispensary that complies with local zoning laws and regulatory guidelines regarding proximity to schools, parks, and other dispensaries. The chosen location must also meet security and accessibility requirements, ensuring a safe and welcoming environment for patients.

Financial readiness is a significant aspect of the pre-application process. Applicants must demonstrate that they have the necessary financial resources to establish and operate the dispensary. This may involve securing funding, providing proof of assets, or demonstrating a stable financial history. The ability to navigate the financial complexities of the medical marijuana industry, including challenges related to banking and taxation, is essential for success.

Background checks are a standard pre-application requirement for dispensary operators and key employees. These checks help to ensure that individuals involved in the dispensary have no criminal history that would disqualify them from participating in the medical marijuana industry. The integrity and trustworthiness of dispensary operators are paramount, given the sensitive nature of the business and the need to prevent diversion and abuse.

Community engagement and support can play a role in the pre-application process. Some jurisdictions require applicants to demonstrate how they will engage with and contribute to their local communities. This might involve plans for educational programs, community service initiatives, or partnerships with local health organizations.

Demonstrating a commitment to positive community impact can be an important aspect of preparing to apply for a dispensary license.

The pre-application requirements for opening a medical marijuana dispensary are designed to ensure that applicants are thoroughly prepared, financially stable, and fully informed about the regulatory landscape. By meeting these requirements, applicants can position themselves for success in the competitive and rapidly evolving medical marijuana industry.

Submitting Your Application

Submitting an application to open a medical marijuana dispensary is a critical and often complex step that requires careful preparation and attention to detail. This phase follows the completion of pre-application requirements and marks the formal entry of the applicant into the regulatory review process. The application process is designed to evaluate the applicant's ability to comply with stringent regulatory standards, ensuring that only qualified entities are granted the privilege to operate within this highly regulated space.

The process begins with the compilation of a comprehensive application package, which typically includes the detailed business plan, financial documents, background check results, security plans, and any other requirements outlined by the regulatory body. The business plan plays a central role in this package, showcasing the applicant's understanding of the industry, market analysis, operational plans, and long-term viability. It must detail how the dispensary will source its products, maintain quality control, ensure patient privacy and security, and comply with all state and local regulations.

Financial documents are another critical component of the application package. Applicants must demonstrate financial stability and the ability to sustain operations over time. This may include bank statements, proof of assets or investments, and detailed financial projections. For many regulators, ensuring that applicants have the financial means to start and maintain their business without resorting to illegal or unethical practices is paramount.

Background checks for all owners, partners, and key employees must be included to satisfy regulators that the business will be managed by individuals with integrity and a clean legal record. This requirement underscores the industry's sensitivity and the need to maintain a secure and trustworthy operation.

Security plans are essential given the value of the products and the cash-heavy nature of the industry. Applicants must outline how they will secure their inventory and premises and ensure the safety of employees and patients. This includes details on surveillance systems, access controls, product tracking mechanisms, and procedures for handling theft or breaches.

Local zoning approvals and evidence of compliance with local laws, such as community support or non-objection letters, may also be required. These documents demonstrate that the dispensary will not face legal challenges related to its location or operation from the local community.

Once the application package is complete, it must be submitted according to the specific guidelines set by the regulatory authority, which may include online submission portals, specific formatting requirements, or physical submission of documents. Paying attention to these details is crucial to avoid delays or rejection.

Application fees, often substantial, must be paid at the time of submission. These fees cover the cost of the regulatory review process and are typically non-refundable, emphasizing the need for applicants to ensure their application is as strong as possible before submission.

After submission, the application enters a review phase, where regulatory officials thoroughly examine every detail of the proposal to ensure compliance with all legal and regulatory standards. This process can take several months and may require applicants to provide additional information, clarify certain aspects of their plan, or participate in interviews or hearings.

Throughout this process, applicants must remain patient and responsive. The ability to quickly and effectively address any concerns raised by regulators can significantly impact the application's success. Moreover, staying informed about any changes in regulations or requirements during the review period is crucial, as these could affect the application's outcome.

Submitting an application for a medical marijuana dispensary license is a demanding process that tests the applicant's commitment, understanding of the industry, and ability to meet rigorous standards. Success in this phase moves the applicant one step closer to entering the medical marijuana market, but it requires meticulous preparation, transparency, and a proactive approach to compliance and regulation.

Post-Application Steps

After submitting an application to open a medical marijuana dispensary, the journey towards launching and operating your business enters a critical phase. This post-application period is marked by anticipation, preparation, and engagement with regulatory bodies, as applicants await the outcome of their submission. Understanding the steps that follow the application submission is crucial for maintaining momentum and ensuring readiness for the next stages.

Once an application is submitted, it enters a review process conducted by the regulatory authority overseeing medical marijuana dispensaries. This review process can be lengthy, often taking several months, as it involves a thorough examination of the application to ensure compliance with all legal and regulatory standards. During this time, applicants may be required to provide additional information or clarification on various aspects of their proposal. Being responsive and cooperative during this phase is essential, as it demonstrates your commitment to compliance and your readiness to operate within the regulatory framework.

While awaiting the review outcome, it's wise for applicants to continue refining their business plan and operational strategies. This might involve finalizing relationships with suppliers, further developing security and safety protocols, or enhancing patient service plans. Preparing for the practical aspects of opening and running a dispensary ensures that once a license is granted, the business can hit the ground running.

Applicants should also take this time to engage with the community where the dispensary will be located. Building positive relationships with local residents, businesses, and healthcare providers can be invaluable for garnering support and integrating the dispensary into the community. Community engagement efforts might include informational meetings, participation in local events, or initiatives that demonstrate the dispensary's commitment to public health and safety.

Another important post-application step is to prepare the physical location of the dispensary. If you have already secured a location, this period can be used to design and renovate the space to meet regulatory requirements and create a welcoming environment for patients.

This includes implementing the necessary security measures, ensuring accessibility, and designing a layout that facilitates efficient operations and patient privacy.

Staff recruitment and training is another critical aspect of the post-application phase. Identifying and hiring qualified staff who share the dispensary's commitment to patient care and compliance is crucial. Providing comprehensive training on product knowledge, regulatory compliance, customer service, and security protocols will ensure that your team is prepared to meet the needs of patients and operate within the legal framework from day one.

Staying informed about regulatory developments and industry trends during the post-application phase is also essential. Regulations governing medical marijuana dispensaries can evolve, and being proactive in adapting to changes demonstrates a commitment to compliance and industry best practices. Additionally, understanding industry trends can inform product selection, marketing strategies, and patient education efforts.

Once a license is granted, there are still several regulatory hurdles to clear before opening. This may include obtaining additional permits, passing final inspections, and completing any required registrations. Ensuring that all regulatory requirements are met before opening is essential for a smooth launch and successful operation.

The post-application phase is a time of preparation, engagement, and vigilance for applicants of medical marijuana dispensaries. It offers an opportunity to lay the groundwork for a successful business, build relationships with the community, and ensure readiness to operate within the regulatory framework. By approaching this phase with diligence and foresight, applicants can position themselves for success in the competitive and evolving medical marijuana industry.

Market Research and Business Planning

Embarking on the journey of opening a medical marijuana dispensary requires thorough market research and meticulous business planning. This foundational step is critical not only for securing a license but also for ensuring the long-term success and sustainability of the business. Market research and business planning are intertwined processes where the insights gained from research directly inform the development of a comprehensive business plan.

Market research in the context of a medical marijuana dispensary involves a deep dive into understanding the local and broader cannabis market, identifying potential patients, analyzing competitors, and keeping abreast of regulatory changes. This research aims to uncover the specific needs and preferences of the target market, the competitive landscape, and potential barriers to entry. Conducting surveys, analyzing industry reports, and engaging with the community can provide valuable insights into consumer behavior, market trends, and unmet needs. Understanding the demographics, conditions treated, and consumption preferences of potential patients can help tailor the product offerings and services to meet market demands.

Additionally, regulatory research is a crucial component of market research, providing insight into the legal framework, licensing requirements, and compliance standards. This research ensures that the business plan aligns with state and local regulations, reducing the risk of legal complications.

Armed with comprehensive market research data, the next step is to develop a detailed business plan. This document serves as a roadmap for establishing and growing the dispensary, outlining the business's mission, vision, and objectives. It begins with an executive summary, which provides a snapshot of the business and its strategic direction. The business plan then delves into the business model, describing how the dispensary will operate, the products and services offered, and how it will generate revenue.

A significant section of the business plan is dedicated to market analysis, incorporating the findings from the initial market research. This section outlines the target market's characteristics, the competitive landscape, and market positioning strategies. It highlights the dispensary's unique value proposition and how it intends to differentiate itself from competitors.

The operational plan is another critical component, detailing the day-to-day operations of the dispensary. This includes the location, facilities, supply chain management, inventory control, patient services, and security measures. The operational plan also outlines the organizational structure, detailing roles and responsibilities, staffing requirements, and management practices.

Financial projections are a cornerstone of the business plan, providing a forecast of the dispensary's financial performance. This includes startup costs, operating expenses, revenue projections, and profitability analysis. Financial projections should be realistic and based on sound assumptions, demonstrating the financial viability of the business to investors and regulators.

Marketing and sales strategies are also outlined in the business plan, detailing how the dispensary will attract and retain patients. This includes branding, advertising, patient education programs, and community engagement initiatives. The marketing plan should align with the regulatory environment, ensuring compliance with advertising and promotional restrictions.

The business plan addresses risk management, identifying potential risks and outlining strategies to mitigate them. This includes regulatory risks, market risks, and operational risks, providing a contingency plan to navigate challenges.

Market research and business planning are indispensable steps in opening a medical marijuana dispensary. They provide a foundation for making informed decisions, securing funding, obtaining a license, and guiding the business towards success. A well-researched and carefully crafted business plan demonstrates professionalism, preparedness, and a deep understanding of the medical marijuana industry, setting the stage for a successful entry into this dynamic and growing market.

Analyzing the Market Demand for Medical Marijuana

Analyzing the market demand for medical marijuana is a critical step for entrepreneurs looking to enter the industry or expand their existing operations. This analysis provides a comprehensive understanding of the current market landscape, including patient needs, industry trends, and competitive dynamics. It involves a multifaceted approach, examining various factors such as legal developments, demographic shifts, consumer behavior, and the broader healthcare context.

The legal status of medical marijuana in a given jurisdiction is a fundamental starting point for analyzing market demand. Legalization not only opens up the market but also shapes its size and characteristics. Changes in legislation can lead to increased patient access, influence public perception, and drive demand. Therefore, staying informed about legal developments and understanding the regulatory framework is crucial for accurately assessing the market potential.

Demographic analysis is another essential component of understanding market demand. This involves identifying the patient population that can benefit from medical marijuana, which may include individuals with chronic pain, epilepsy, multiple sclerosis, and other qualifying conditions. Demographic trends, such as an aging population or increasing prevalence of certain medical conditions, can influence the demand for medical marijuana. Analyzing demographic data helps in estimating the size of the target market and understanding patient needs and preferences.

Consumer behavior and attitudes towards medical marijuana also play a significant role in market demand. This includes patient openness to using cannabis as a treatment option, perceived effectiveness, and preferences for different product forms, such as edibles, tinctures, or topical applications. Surveys, focus groups, and market research studies can provide valuable insights into consumer behavior, helping to identify market segments and tailor product offerings accordingly.

The broader healthcare context is another critical factor in analyzing market demand for medical marijuana. This includes the availability of alternative treatments, the stance of the medical community on cannabis use, and insurance coverage considerations. Understanding how medical marijuana fits into the overall treatment landscape is essential for assessing its potential market demand. Collaboration with healthcare providers and patient advocacy groups can offer insights into how medical marijuana is perceived and used within the healthcare system.

Competitive analysis is also a vital part of understanding market demand. Identifying existing dispensaries, their product offerings, pricing strategies, and market positioning can provide a clearer picture of the competitive landscape. This analysis helps in identifying gaps in the market, understanding competitive advantages, and developing strategies to differentiate one's business from others.

Analyzing economic factors, such as pricing trends, supply chain dynamics, and the impact of taxation, is important for understanding market demand. Economic considerations can affect patient access to medical marijuana and influence consumer choices, especially in markets where patients must pay out-of-pocket for their medication.

Analyzing the market demand for medical marijuana involves a comprehensive approach that considers legal, demographic, consumer behavior, healthcare, competitive, and economic factors. By gaining a deep understanding of these elements, entrepreneurs and business owners can make informed decisions about entering the market, expanding operations, and tailoring their product and service offerings to meet the needs of medical marijuana patients. This analysis is not only critical for business success but also for contributing to the broader goal of improving patient access to effective treatment options.

Identifying Your Target Market

Identifying your target market within the medical marijuana industry involves a nuanced understanding of the diverse patient demographics, conditions treated, and consumer preferences. This process is critical for tailoring product offerings, marketing strategies, and customer service to meet the specific needs of different patient groups. By focusing on the unique characteristics and needs of your target market, you can more effectively position your dispensary or product line, ensuring that you address the demands of those most likely to benefit from medical marijuana.

The first step in identifying your target market is to understand the legal qualifications for medical marijuana use in your jurisdiction. Different states or countries have varying lists of qualifying medical conditions that can legally be treated with cannabis. Common conditions include chronic pain, multiple sclerosis, epilepsy, glaucoma, and chemotherapy-induced nausea, among others. By reviewing these conditions, you can begin to outline the patient profiles that are most likely to seek out your products or services.

Demographic factors play a crucial role in defining your target market. Age, gender, and socioeconomic status can all influence a patient's likelihood to use medical marijuana, as well as their preferences for certain types of products (e.g., edibles vs. vaporizers) or strains. For example, older patients might be interested in non-smoke-able forms of cannabis that are perceived as being more health-conscious, such as tinctures or topical. Understanding these demographic nuances allows for more effective marketing and product development.

Lifestyle and consumer behavior are also important considerations. Some patients may prioritize convenience and discretion, preferring products that are easy to use and carry. Others may value organic or sustainably grown cannabis products, reflecting broader lifestyle choices around health and wellness.

Identifying lifestyle patterns and consumer behaviors can help refine marketing messages and product lines to appeal to specific segments within the broader market.

Geographic location is another key factor in identifying your target market. The local culture and attitudes towards cannabis, the prevalence of qualifying medical conditions, and even the local climate can impact patient needs and product demand. For instance, dispensaries in areas with a higher concentration of veterans might see more demand for PTSD-related treatments, while those in regions with older populations might focus more on products aimed at chronic pain or arthritis.

Analyzing competitive landscapes and existing market gaps can help in identifying underserved or niche patient groups. This might include patients with rare medical conditions, those seeking specific cannabis strains or products not widely available, or communities that have been historically underserved by the medical cannabis industry. By targeting these markets, businesses can differentiate themselves from competitors and build a loyal customer base.

Identifying your target market in the medical marijuana industry requires a multi-faceted approach that considers legal qualifications, demographic factors, lifestyle and consumer behavior, geographic location, and competitive landscapes.

This strategic focus not only enhances business viability but also ensures that patients receive the products and services that best meet their medical needs and personal preferences.

Competitive Analysis

Competitive analysis in the context of the medical marijuana industry is an in-depth examination of the existing marketplace to understand the strengths, weaknesses, opportunities, and threats presented by other businesses operating within the same space. This analysis is crucial for any dispensary or business looking to establish itself or grow in the medical marijuana sector, as it provides invaluable insights into market trends, consumer preferences, and the competitive landscape.

At its core, competitive analysis involves identifying the key players in the medical marijuana market, which includes other dispensaries, cultivation operations, and ancillary businesses that contribute to the industry's ecosystem. This step is not just about listing competitors but understanding their market position, brand identity, product offerings, pricing strategies, customer service approaches, and marketing tactics. Such an understanding allows a business to gauge the competitive intensity and dynamics of the industry.

A thorough competitive analysis goes beyond surface-level observations to delve into the operational aspects of competing businesses. This includes evaluating the quality and variety of products offered, such as different strains of cannabis, edibles, tinctures, and topicals, as well as services like patient education and consultation. Understanding how competitors differentiate themselves in terms of product quality, innovation, and customer experience can highlight gaps in the market that a new entrant might fill or areas where an existing business can improve.

Pricing strategies of competitors are also a critical component of the analysis. By examining how competitors price their products and services, a business can identify pricing trends within the industry, consumer sensitivity to price changes, and opportunities for competitive pricing strategies that can attract price-conscious consumers without sacrificing profit margins.

Marketing and customer engagement strategies employed by competitors offer insights into how they build brand awareness, attract new customers, and retain existing ones. This includes analyzing online presence, social media activity, advertising campaigns, loyalty programs, and community involvement. Understanding these strategies helps in crafting more effective marketing campaigns that resonate with the target audience and foster a loyal customer base.

Competitive analysis involves assessing the regulatory compliance and operational efficiency of competitors. This aspect includes how well competitors navigate the complex legal landscape of the medical marijuana industry, adhere to regulatory requirements, manage supply chain logistics, and utilize technology for operations and customer engagement. Identifying best practices and areas of vulnerability among competitors can inform operational improvements and risk management strategies.

The ultimate goal of conducting a competitive analysis is to identify opportunities and threats in the marketplace. Opportunities may arise from unmet customer needs, underserved market segments, or technological advancements that can be leveraged to gain a competitive edge. Threats might include regulatory changes, market saturation, or aggressive competitive tactics. By understanding these opportunities and threats, businesses can develop strategic plans that focus on differentiation, market positioning, and sustainable growth.

Competitive analysis in the medical marijuana industry is about gaining a comprehensive understanding of the competitive landscape to make informed strategic decisions. It enables businesses to identify their unique value proposition, optimize their operations, and craft strategies that address the needs and preferences of their target market while navigating the challenges of a highly regulated and competitive industry.

This analysis is not a one-time effort but an ongoing process that helps businesses stay agile, responsive to market changes, and ahead of the competition.

Crafting a Detailed Business Plan

Crafting a detailed business plan for a medical marijuana dispensary is an essential step towards establishing a successful and sustainable operation. This document serves as a roadmap, outlining the business's objectives, strategies, market position, financial projections, and operational plans. It is a critical tool for attracting investors, securing financing, and guiding the day-to-day management of the business.

The process of crafting a detailed business plan starts with a clear articulation of the business's vision and mission. This involves defining the core values of the dispensary, its overarching goals, and the specific needs it aims to address within the medical marijuana market. This section sets the tone for the business plan, establishing the foundation upon which the rest of the document is built.

Next, a thorough market analysis is conducted to understand the dynamics of the medical marijuana industry within the target market. This analysis covers the legal and regulatory environment, the size and demographics of the potential patient base, current and anticipated market trends, and a detailed competitive analysis. The goal is to identify opportunities and challenges in the market and to develop strategies that leverage these insights to create a competitive advantage.

The business plan then delves into the organization and management structure of the dispensary. This section outlines the ownership structure, the qualifications and roles of the management team, and the operational framework that will support the dispensary's day-to-day activities. It is important to demonstrate that the team has the expertise, experience, and leadership skills necessary to navigate the complexities of the medical marijuana industry successfully.

A critical component of the business plan is the marketing and sales strategy. This section describes how the dispensary intends to attract and retain patients, including branding, advertising, patient education programs, and loyalty initiatives. It also covers the dispensary's product strategy, detailing the range of products that will be offered, pricing strategies, and how these products meet the needs and preferences of the target patient demographic.

The operational plan provides an in-depth look at the day-to-day operations of the dispensary. This includes the procurement of products, inventory management, and compliance with regulatory requirements, security measures, and customer service protocols. The operational plan should outline the processes and systems that will be in place to ensure a smooth, efficient, and compliant operation.

Financial projections are a crucial element of the business plan, providing a detailed forecast of the dispensary's financial performance over a specified period. This section includes income statements, cash flow statements, and balance sheets, as well as a break-even analysis. Assumptions made in the financial model should be clearly stated and realistic. This section demonstrates the financial viability of the business and its potential for profitability.

The business plan should address any risks and challenges that the dispensary may face and outline strategies for mitigating these risks. This could include changes in regulatory policies, competition, market saturation, or shifts in consumer behavior. Demonstrating an understanding of potential obstacles and having a contingency plan in place shows foresight and preparedness.

Crafting a detailed business plan for a medical marijuana dispensary involves a comprehensive analysis of the market, a clear definition of the business's goals and strategies, and a realistic assessment of its financial prospects. This document is not only a blueprint for the operation of the business but also a crucial tool for communicating its vision and potential to stakeholders, investors, and regulatory bodies.

Executive Summary

The Executive Summary of a business plan plays a crucial role as it provides a concise overview of the entire document, encapsulating the most critical points and drawing the reader in to learn more about the venture. This section is often the first part of the business plan that investors, lenders, and other stakeholders read, making it vital for capturing their interest and conveying the essence of the business succinctly and effectively.

Crafting an Executive Summary involves summarizing the key aspects of the business plan, including the business concept, market analysis, unique value proposition, financial highlights, and the strategic direction of the venture. Despite being a summary, it needs to be compelling and comprehensive enough to stand on its own, providing all necessary information at a glance.

The Executive Summary begins by introducing the business idea. This includes a brief description of the medical marijuana dispensary, the products and services offered, and the specific needs it aims to address within the market. It sets the stage by outlining the vision and mission of the dispensary, giving readers a clear understanding of the purpose and goals of the business.

Following the introduction, the summary highlights the opportunity in the market that the dispensary intends to capitalize on. This involves a brief overview of the market analysis, touching on the demand for medical marijuana, the target demographic, and the competitive landscape. It succinctly explains why there is a need for the dispensary and how it will meet that need differently or better than existing competitors.

The unique value proposition of the dispensary is then outlined, detailing what sets the business apart from others in the market. This could include proprietary products, superior customer service, innovative technology, or a strong focus on community engagement. The goal is to convey the competitive edge that will drive the success of the dispensary.

Financial highlights are an essential part of the Executive Summary, providing a snapshot of the projected financial performance of the dispensary. This section includes key figures such as startup costs, revenue projections, profitability timelines, and funding requirements. It gives readers a quick overview of the financial viability and investment potential of the business.

The strategic direction of the dispensary is also addressed, outlining the key strategies that will be employed to achieve the business's goals. This might include marketing strategies, expansion plans, or partnerships that will be leveraged to grow the business.

The summary should convey a sense of how the dispensary plans to navigate the market and scale its operations.

The Executive Summary concludes with a call to action, encouraging readers to delve deeper into the business plan for more detailed information. It may also include a statement of request, outlining the specific funding or support the business is seeking and inviting potential investors or partners to engage further with the venture.

The Executive Summary is a microcosm of the business plan, offering a clear, engaging, and compelling overview of the business opportunity. It requires careful crafting to ensure that it captures the essence of the business, highlights its potential for success, and motivates readers to invest their time, resources, or support in the venture.

Company Description

The Company Description section of a business plan offers a detailed overview of the medical marijuana dispensary, providing readers with a comprehensive understanding of what the business does, the market it serves, the specific needs it addresses, and how it distinguishes itself from competitors. This segment is crucial for setting the context of the business plan, enabling stakeholders, investors, and other interested parties to grasp the essence and scope of the dispensary's operations.

Starting with the basics, the Company Description outlines the business's legal name, location, and the structure of the company, whether it's a sole proprietorship, partnership, LLC, or corporation. This information establishes the legal and logistical foundation of the dispensary, giving readers a sense of its operational framework and geographic footprint.

Following the foundational details, the description delves into the history and background of the dispensary. This narrative can include the inspiration behind the business, its founding story, key milestones achieved to date, and any significant challenges overcome. This backstory not only humanizes the business but also demonstrates the founders' commitment, resilience, and vision, which can be particularly compelling to potential investors and partners.

The core of the Company Description is a detailed explanation of the products and services offered by the dispensary. This encompasses the range of medical marijuana products, such as flower, edibles, concentrates, topicals, and tinctures, as well as any ancillary services provided, like patient education, consultation services, and delivery options. The description highlights the quality, sourcing, and unique attributes of the products, underscoring the dispensary's commitment to patient care and product excellence.

A critical component of the Company Description is the identification of the target market. This section details the demographic and psychographic profile of the dispensary's ideal customer base, including age, medical conditions, lifestyle preferences, and consumption habits. Understanding the target market enables the business to tailor its products, services, and marketing efforts to meet the specific needs and preferences of its patients.

The Company Description also addresses the market need the dispensary aims to fulfill. This could involve addressing a lack of access to high-quality medical marijuana products, offering specialized products for specific medical conditions, or providing a superior customer experience. By clearly articulating the problem or gap in the market, the dispensary positions itself as a solution-oriented business focused on meeting patient needs.

Differentiation is another crucial aspect of the Company Description. This section elaborates on what sets the dispensary apart from its competitors, whether it's through innovative product offerings, exceptional service, community involvement, or a unique brand identity. Highlighting these differentiators is key to establishing the dispensary's unique value proposition and competitive edge in the market.

The Company Description outlines the business's goals and objectives, providing a clear sense of direction for the future. This may include short-term goals, such as expanding the product line or opening additional locations, as well as long-term objectives, like becoming a market leader in medical marijuana or advancing cannabis research. By articulating these goals, the business conveys its ambition, strategy, and commitment to growth and innovation.

The Company Description is a vital component of the business plan, offering a detailed and compelling overview of the medical marijuana dispensary. It provides the foundational information necessary for understanding the business, while also showcasing its mission, market positioning, and strategic direction.

This section sets the stage for the rest of the business plan, highlighting the dispensary's potential for success and its commitment to serving the needs of its patients.

Market Analysis

The Market Analysis section of a business plan is a comprehensive examination of the industry, market trends, target demographics, competition, and the regulatory environment. It's pivotal for understanding the landscape within which a medical marijuana dispensary operates, assessing the potential for growth, and identifying strategies to capture and expand market share. This analysis not only demonstrates the business's market knowledge but also its potential to succeed in a competitive and ever-evolving industry.

At the outset, the Market Analysis delves into the medical marijuana industry at large, examining its current state, growth trends, and future projections. This overview provides a macro perspective on the industry, highlighting factors driving growth, such as legislative changes, shifts in public perception, and advancements in cannabis research. Understanding the industry's trajectory helps in positioning the dispensary for future growth and aligning its offerings with market demands.

Following the industry overview, the analysis narrows down to specific market trends that could impact the dispensary's operations. This includes trends in consumer behavior, product innovation, and technological advancements in cannabis cultivation and product development. By staying attuned to these trends, the dispensary can anticipate changes in consumer preferences, adapt its product lineup, and leverage technology to enhance efficiency and customer experience.

The Market Analysis also requires a deep dive into the target market, defining the demographics, psychographics, and consumption patterns of the dispensary's potential customer base. This segment of the analysis considers factors such as age, gender, medical conditions, and lifestyle choices that influence cannabis consumption. Understanding the target market at this granular level enables the dispensary to tailor its marketing strategies, product offerings, and customer service approaches to meet the specific needs and preferences of its patients.

A critical component of the Market Analysis is the competitive landscape. This involves identifying existing dispensaries and other competitors within the target market, assessing their strengths and weaknesses, market share, and positioning.

The analysis should cover the range of products offered by competitors, their pricing strategies, marketing approaches, and customer service practices. By evaluating the competition, the dispensary can identify gaps in the market, differentiate itself from other players, and develop strategies to attract and retain customers.

Regulatory considerations are an integral part of the Market Analysis. The legal and regulatory framework governing medical marijuana varies by jurisdiction and has a significant impact on dispensary operations. The analysis should address current regulations, potential legislative changes, and compliance requirements. Understanding the regulatory environment is crucial for mitigating risks, ensuring compliance, and positioning the dispensary as a responsible and trusted player in the medical marijuana market.

The Market Analysis outlines the opportunities and challenges within the market. Opportunities might include underserved patient demographics, emerging trends in cannabis consumption, or gaps in the product offerings of existing competitors. Challenges could encompass regulatory hurdles, market saturation, or shifts in consumer behavior. Identifying these opportunities and challenges enables the dispensary to develop strategic initiatives that capitalize on market potential while navigating potential obstacles.

In essence, the Market Analysis section of a business plan provides a detailed and nuanced understanding of the medical marijuana market. It equips the dispensary with the insights needed to make informed business decisions, tailor its offerings to meet market demands, and develop competitive strategies that ensure long-term growth and success in the industry.

Organization and Management

The Organization and Management section of a business plan details the operational structure and leadership of a medical marijuana dispensary, laying out how the business is structured, who is in charge, and what their qualifications are. This segment is crucial for potential investors and stakeholders as it provides insight into the dispensary's governance, operational efficiency, and the expertise behind its operations, showcasing the team's ability to navigate the complexities of the medical marijuana industry successfully.

This section typically starts by presenting the business structure, whether it's a sole proprietorship, partnership, limited liability company (LLC), or corporation. This choice affects taxation, liability, and regulatory considerations, making it a fundamental aspect of how the business operates.

The legal structure chosen for the dispensary reflects the owners' approach to risk, control, and their vision for growth and scalability. It also sets the groundwork for how decisions are made and how profits and losses are shared.

Following the business structure, a detailed breakdown of the management team and their roles within the organization is provided. This includes information about the founders, board of directors, and key employees, highlighting their backgrounds, experience, and specific qualifications relevant to their roles in the dispensary. For each key member, a mini-biography that includes their educational background, previous industry experience, and any specific achievements or skills that contribute to their ability to add value to the business is presented. This not only establishes credibility but also reassures investors and stakeholders of the team's capability to manage the dispensary effectively.

The Organization and Management section also often includes an organizational chart that visually represents the company's structure. This chart shows the hierarchy within the dispensary and how different roles and departments interact, providing clarity on reporting lines and responsibilities. For a medical marijuana dispensary, this might include the retail operations, procurement, compliance, marketing, and customer service departments, among others.

The organizational chart helps stakeholders understand the workflow and how the dispensary ensures efficient operations and compliance with regulatory requirements.

In addition to outlining the current management team and organizational structure, this section may also discuss any gaps in the team and how the company plans to fill these positions. This forward-looking approach indicates the dispensary's growth strategy and its readiness to scale operations by attracting talent that can address future challenges and opportunities.

Moreover, the section can highlight the governance practices of the dispensary, including advisory boards or consultants who provide expertise on medical marijuana, legal compliance, healthcare, or business strategy. This further demonstrates the dispensary's commitment to best practices, regulatory compliance, and continuous improvement.

For investors, the Organization and Management section of the business plan is a critical determinant of the dispensary's potential for success. It showcases not just who is running the business but how it is run, reflecting on the dispensary's professionalism, operational efficiency, and the strategic approach to achieving its goals. By providing a clear and comprehensive overview of the dispensary's leadership and organizational structure, this section helps build confidence among potential investors and partners in the management team's ability to navigate the complexities of the medical marijuana industry and drive the business towards sustainable growth and profitability.

Sales Strategies

The Sales Strategies section of a business plan outlines how a medical marijuana dispensary intends to generate revenue, attract and retain customers, and achieve its sales targets. This component is vital for illustrating the business's approach to navigating the competitive landscape, understanding customer needs, and leveraging its strengths to capture market share. Effective sales strategies are tailored to the specific context of the medical marijuana industry, taking into account regulatory constraints, patient needs, and the evolving marketplace.

The sales strategy for a medical marijuana dispensary begins with a clear understanding of the target market. This involves identifying the patient demographics most likely to benefit from the dispensary's products, such as individuals with chronic pain, anxiety, or other conditions that medical marijuana can alleviate. By focusing on specific patient groups, the dispensary can tailor its marketing messages, product offerings, and customer service to meet these patients' unique needs and preferences.

Product differentiation is another key aspect of the sales strategy. Given the wide range of products available in the medical marijuana market, from various strains of cannabis to edibles, tinctures, and topicals, a dispensary must clearly communicate the benefits and unique features of its products. This might involve emphasizing organic cultivation practices, the availability of rare or specialized strains, or the development of proprietary products that address specific health concerns. Product differentiation helps in establishing the dispensary's brand and attracting patients looking for specific solutions.

Pricing strategies also play a crucial role in the sales approach. Dispensaries must balance the need to be competitive with the necessity of covering costs and achieving profitability. Pricing strategies might include tiered pricing for different quality levels, discounts for veterans or low-income patients, loyalty programs, or promotions for first-time patients. A well-considered pricing strategy not only attracts customers but also builds loyalty and encourages repeat business.

Customer experience is at the heart of effective sales strategies for medical marijuana dispensaries. This encompasses everything from the physical layout of the dispensary and the professionalism of the staff to the ease of the purchasing process and the quality of after-sales support. Providing a safe, welcoming, and educational environment for patients, especially those new to medical marijuana, can differentiate a dispensary in a crowded market. Training staff to be knowledgeable and compassionate, offering private consultations, and ensuring discretion are all elements that contribute to a positive customer experience.

Digital marketing and online sales are increasingly important components of a dispensary's sales strategy. With many patients turning to the internet to research medical marijuana options, having a strong online presence is crucial. This might include an informative website, active social media profiles, and email marketing campaigns. For dispensaries in jurisdictions where it's permitted, offering online ordering for in-store pickup or delivery can provide added convenience for patients and drive sales.

Community engagement and education can support the dispensary's sales strategies by building trust and establishing the business as a reliable source of information on medical marijuana. Hosting educational events, participating in health fairs, and partnering with local healthcare providers can help raise awareness of the dispensary and its products, driving patient referrals and increasing sales.

The sales strategies for a medical marijuana dispensary must be multifaceted, combining a deep understanding of the target market with product differentiation, competitive pricing, exceptional customer service, and effective use of digital marketing. By focusing on these areas, a dispensary can attract and retain patients, achieve its sales targets, and build a strong position in the competitive medical marijuana market.

Funding Request

In the Funding Request section of a business plan, a medical marijuana dispensary outlines its financial needs to potential investors or lenders, detailing the amount of funding required, the intended use of these funds, and the proposed terms for financing. This section is crucial for securing the capital necessary to start or expand the dispensary's operations, highlighting the business's understanding of its financial needs and its strategy for using external funding to achieve growth and profitability.

The Funding Request starts with a clear statement of the total amount of capital needed. This figure is derived from the detailed financial projections included elsewhere in the business plan, such as startup costs, operating expenses, and projected cash flow shortfalls. By specifying the amount, the dispensary demonstrates a precise understanding of its financial requirements, lending credibility to its request.

Following the statement of need, the section breaks down how the requested funds will be utilized. This breakdown covers various categories of expenses, including but not limited to, initial setup costs (e.g., leasehold improvements, equipment purchases), inventory acquisition, marketing and branding activities, staffing and operational costs, and contingency reserves. Providing a detailed allocation of funds reassures investors and lenders that the dispensary has a well-thought-out plan for utilizing their capital effectively and efficiently.

The Funding Request also addresses the timing of the funding needs, outlining when different segments of the capital will be required. This schedule aligns with the dispensary's operational milestones and growth plans, ensuring that funds are available as needed to support the business's development trajectory. Understanding the timing helps investors and lenders assess the urgency and phasing of the funding request, facilitating their decision-making process.

In addition to detailing the amount, use, and timing of the funding, the section outlines the proposed terms of financing. This might include the desired mix of debt and equity financing, interest rates and equity dilution expectations, repayment schedules for loans, and any specific conditions or covenants the dispensary is willing to accept. For equity investors, information on the proposed valuation of the business and the equity stake being offered in exchange for funding is crucial. By specifying these terms, the dispensary initiates the negotiation process with potential financiers, setting the stage for further discussions.

The Funding Request also highlights the expected impact of the funding on the dispensary's financial performance and growth prospects. This includes projections of revenue growth, profitability improvements, and the achievement of critical business milestones that the funding will enable. Demonstrating the positive financial implications of the requested funding helps to justify the investment or loan, showing potential financiers the return on their capital.

This section reiterates the dispensary's value proposition, competitive advantages, and market opportunities, tying these elements back to the financial request. It makes a compelling case for why investing in or lending to the dispensary presents a favorable opportunity, given the business's potential for success and the strategic use of the requested funds to capitalize on market opportunities.

The Funding Request section of a business plan is a direct appeal to potential investors and lenders, articulating the medical marijuana dispensary's financial needs in a detailed, transparent, and strategic manner. It plays a critical role in securing the external capital necessary for launching or expanding the dispensary, underpinning the business's path to growth and profitability.

Financial Projections

In the context of a business plan for a medical marijuana dispensary, the Financial Projections section is pivotal for demonstrating the venture's potential for profitability and financial stability over a specified timeframe. This section outlines the expected financial performance of the dispensary, including revenue forecasts, cost estimates, profitability timelines, and cash flow projections. By presenting a clear and realistic picture of the dispensary's financial future, this section helps investors, lenders, and other stakeholders assess the viability and investment worthiness of the business.

Financial projections typically cover a period of three to five years and are grounded in a combination of historical data (if available), industry benchmarks, and assumptions about future market conditions.

The projections are broken down into several key components:

1. Revenue Projections: This part estimates the dispensary's sales over the projection period. It is based on a thorough analysis of the target market, product offerings, pricing strategies, and sales and marketing plans. Revenue projections should account for factors such as market growth, competition, and regulatory changes that could impact sales. They often include best-case, worst-case, and most likely scenarios to provide a range of possible outcomes.

2. Cost of Goods Sold (COGS): COGS estimates the direct costs associated with the production and procurement of the dispensary's products, such as purchasing cannabis from growers, manufacturing edibles, or packaging and labeling costs. Understanding COGS is crucial for assessing the gross margin and for pricing strategies.

3. Operating Expenses: This section details the expected costs of running the dispensary, excluding COGS. It includes expenses such as rent, utilities, salaries and wages, marketing and advertising costs, insurance, and compliance-related expenses. Breaking down

operating expenses helps in identifying areas for cost control and efficiency improvements.

4. Profitability Analysis: The profitability analysis combines revenue projections with COGS and operating expenses to forecast the dispensary's net profit or loss over the projection period. This analysis is critical for determining when the dispensary expects to break even and achieve profitability, providing insight into the business's long-term financial health.

5. Cash Flow Projections: Cash flow projections provide an overview of the expected inflow and outflow of cash within the dispensary, highlighting periods of potential cash shortfalls or surpluses. This component is essential for managing liquidity, planning for capital expenditures, and ensuring that the dispensary can meet its financial obligations on time.

6. Break-even Analysis: The break-even analysis identifies the point at which total revenues equal total expenses, indicating when the dispensary will start generating a profit. This analysis helps in setting realistic sales targets and evaluating the financial feasibility of the business model.

7. Capital Expenditures and Investments: This subsection outlines expected investments in fixed assets, such as property, equipment, and technology, which are necessary for establishing and expanding

the dispensary's operations. It also includes any plans for future investments to support growth.

Financial projections should be accompanied by a narrative explanation that outlines the assumptions made in developing the forecasts, such as expected market growth rates, pricing strategies, and operational efficiency improvements. This narrative provides context for the projections, helping stakeholders understand the basis for the forecasts and the factors that could impact the dispensary's financial performance.

The Financial Projections section is a critical part of the business plan, offering a detailed and forward-looking view of the dispensary's financial trajectory. It requires careful preparation and a deep understanding of the dispensary's business model, market dynamics, and operational considerations. By presenting realistic and well-supported financial projections, the dispensary can demonstrate its potential for success and attract the necessary funding and support to realize its vision.

Financial Planning and Management

Financial planning and management are critical components for the success of any business, including a medical marijuana dispensary. This process involves forecasting financial needs, managing resources effectively, and ensuring the business remains viable and profitable over time. For a medical marijuana dispensary, where regulatory compliance and market fluctuations can significantly impact operations, astute financial planning and management become even more crucial.

The first step in financial planning involves creating a detailed business plan that includes comprehensive financial projections, as previously discussed. This plan serves as a roadmap, guiding the dispensary through its initial setup, growth phases, and any market challenges. It should outline anticipated costs, potential revenue streams, and profitability timelines, providing a clear picture of financial health and sustainability.

Effective financial management for a dispensary also requires setting up appropriate accounting and financial tracking systems. These systems should be capable of handling the complexities of the cannabis industry, including tracking inventory from seed to sale, managing cash flows in an industry where banking access can be limited, and ensuring compliance with tax regulations specific to the cannabis sector. Implementing robust accounting software and employing professionals with experience in cannabis accounting can help dispensaries navigate these challenges.

Cash flow management is another critical aspect, especially given the cash-intensive nature of the cannabis industry. Dispensaries must carefully monitor cash inflows and outflows, maintain adequate reserves for unexpected expenses, and plan for future investments. Strategies might include optimizing inventory levels to free up cash, negotiating favorable payment terms with suppliers, and carefully timing major expenditures.

Given the legal uncertainties and banking restrictions faced by the cannabis industry, dispensaries must also explore alternative financing options. Traditional bank loans may be inaccessible, so dispensaries might look into private investors, venture capital, or cannabis-specific financing solutions. Crafting a compelling pitch and maintaining transparent, professional financial records increases the likelihood of securing such funding.

Tax planning is another area where dispensaries face unique challenges. The U.S. Internal Revenue Code Section 280E prohibits businesses engaged in the trafficking of Schedule I or II substances from deducting ordinary business expenses, placing a significant financial strain on dispensaries. Effective tax planning, therefore, involves strategies to minimize tax liabilities while remaining compliant with federal laws. This might include optimizing cost of goods sold (COGS) deductions or structuring the business to separate non-cannabis activities that can claim deductions.

Risk management is an essential component of financial planning in the cannabis industry. This includes not only financial risks but also legal, regulatory, and market risks. Dispensaries should implement comprehensive risk management strategies, including insurance coverage tailored to the cannabis industry, compliance programs to avoid regulatory penalties, and market analysis to anticipate and adapt to changes in consumer demand or regulatory environments.

Financial planning and management in a medical marijuana dispensary involve regular review and adjustment of financial strategies. The cannabis industry is rapidly evolving, with frequent changes in laws, market dynamics, and consumer preferences. Dispensaries must regularly review their financial performance, reassess their financial strategies, and adjust their operations accordingly to remain competitive and profitable.

Financial planning and management are foundational to the success of a medical marijuana dispensary. Through meticulous financial forecasting, effective cash flow management, strategic financing, diligent tax planning, comprehensive risk management, and adaptive financial strategies, dispensaries can navigate the complexities of the cannabis industry and achieve sustainable growth and profitability.

Estimating Start-Up Costs

Estimating start-up costs for a medical marijuana dispensary involves a comprehensive analysis of all expenses required to launch and operate the business until it becomes self-sustaining. Start-up costs are critical for planning, securing financing, and ensuring the long-term viability of the dispensary. These costs can vary significantly depending on the location, size of the operation, regulatory requirements, and the level of investment in facilities and inventory.

However, a detailed estimate can provide a solid foundation for the financial planning necessary to navigate the initial stages of setting up a dispensary.

Initial Licensing and Application Fees: One of the first expenses involves the costs associated with obtaining the necessary licenses to operate a medical marijuana dispensary. These fees can vary widely by state and locality and may include costs for background checks, initial application fees, and the license itself. In some jurisdictions, these fees can be substantial, requiring careful budgeting from the outset.

Real Estate and Renovations: Securing a location for the dispensary involves costs such as leasing or purchasing property, which can vary based on market rates in the chosen location. Additionally, most dispensaries require renovations to ensure the space meets specific operational, security, and compliance requirements. This can include the installation of secure display cases, surveillance systems, and secure storage for inventory, as well as customer-facing areas that are welcoming and compliant with accessibility standards.

Inventory Costs: Initial inventory is a significant expense for new dispensaries. This includes purchasing a variety of cannabis products, such as flower, edibles, concentrates, and topicals, to meet the anticipated demand. The cost will vary based on the range of products offered and the volume of inventory purchased upfront. Establishing relationships with reliable suppliers who offer favorable terms can help manage these costs effectively.

Technology and POS Systems: Investing in the right technology is crucial for inventory management, compliance tracking, and sales transactions. This includes purchasing or leasing point-of-sale (POS) systems designed for the cannabis industry, which can handle inventory tracking from seed to sale, ensure compliance with state regulations, and manage customer transactions. Additional technology costs might include computer hardware, software subscriptions, and security systems.

Marketing and Branding: Building a brand and marketing the dispensary to attract customers involve costs such as logo design, website development, social media campaigns, and traditional advertising. Effective marketing is crucial for establishing the dispensary's presence in the market, attracting customers, and building loyalty.

Operational Expenses: Initial operational expenses include utilities, insurance, and salaries for staff. Staffing costs can vary depending on the size of the dispensary and the expertise required, including knowledgeable budtenders, security personnel, and management staff. Comprehensive insurance coverage is also essential to protect against theft, liability, and other risks.

Legal and Professional Fees: Given the complexities of operating within the cannabis industry, legal and consulting fees can be significant. These expenses cover initial legal advice on compliance and regulations, financial consulting, and ongoing compliance monitoring. Engaging with experts who understand the nuances of the cannabis industry is critical for navigating legal hurdles and establishing a compliant operation.

Contingency Fund: Finally, it's prudent to allocate a portion of the start-up budget to a contingency fund. This fund can cover unexpected expenses, delays in the licensing process, or fluctuations in market demand. Having a financial buffer can help new dispensaries manage the uncertainties that come with launching a new business in a highly regulated industry.

Estimating start-up costs with accuracy and realism is essential for the successful launch of a medical marijuana dispensary. It ensures that entrepreneurs have a clear understanding of the financial commitment required, can secure sufficient funding, and have the resources needed to sustain the business through its initial growth phase.

Understanding the Sources of Funding

Understanding the sources of funding is crucial for entrepreneurs looking to start a medical marijuana dispensary. Given the unique challenges and opportunities in the cannabis industry, including legal restrictions and market potential, identifying and securing the right type of funding can significantly impact the success of the business.

Here's an overview of common funding sources for medical marijuana dispensaries, along with considerations unique to the cannabis sector:

Personal Savings: Many entrepreneurs start with their personal savings to fund their business ventures. This method has the advantage of not diluting ownership or accruing debt but may not be sufficient for the high start-up costs associated with dispensaries due to licensing fees, property leases, and inventory.

Friends and Family: Another common source of initial funding comes from friends and family who believe in the business concept. While potentially easier to obtain and more flexible in terms, these arrangements can strain personal relationships if the business does not perform as expected.

Angel Investors: Angel investors are individuals who provide capital for start-ups, often in exchange for ownership equity or convertible debt. In the cannabis industry, some investors specialize in or are open to funding marijuana-related businesses, attracted by the high growth potential. However, they may demand significant control or a high return on investment.

Venture Capital Firms: Similar to angel investors but on a larger scale, venture capital firms provide funding to early-stage, high-potential companies. While more substantial sums of money are available through these firms, they are typically very selective, often seeking businesses with proven models and the potential for rapid growth. Venture capital may be more accessible to dispensaries with a strong operational record and a clear path to significant market share.

Cannabis Business Loans: Some financial institutions and private lenders specialize in the cannabis industry, offering loans tailored to dispensaries. These can cover various needs, from start-up costs to expansion projects. However, interest rates may be higher than standard business loans due to the perceived risk associated with the industry.

Crowdfunding: Platforms that allow businesses to raise small amounts of money from a large number of people have become a popular way to fund start-ups. Cannabis-specific crowdfunding platforms have emerged, enabling dispensaries to raise funds while complying with legal regulations. This method can also serve as a marketing tool, building a community of supporters around the business.

Real Estate Investment Trusts (REITs): For dispensaries that need significant capital for real estate, partnering with a REIT can be an option. Some REITs specialize in properties for the cannabis industry, providing funding in exchange for long-term leases.

Equipment Financing: Dispensaries require specific equipment for operations, from security systems to POS systems. Equipment financing allows businesses to purchase this equipment through loans specifically for this purpose, helping conserve cash for other uses.

When exploring these funding sources, dispensaries must navigate the complexities of the cannabis legal landscape. For instance, traditional banking services and federal funding options are often unavailable due to the federal classification of marijuana as a controlled substance. Therefore, understanding the legal implications and ensuring compliance with both state and federal laws is essential when securing funding.

Preparing a compelling business plan, demonstrating a deep understanding of the market, and showcasing a clear path to profitability are crucial for attracting investors and lenders. As the cannabis industry continues to evolve, so too do the opportunities for funding, requiring entrepreneurs to stay informed and adaptable in their approach to securing the capital necessary for their dispensaries.

Budgeting and Financial Management

Budgeting and financial management are essential practices for the success of a medical marijuana dispensary, given the industry's unique financial challenges, including strict regulatory compliance, taxation issues, and often limited access to traditional banking services. Effective budgeting and financial management not only help in sustaining operations but also in positioning the dispensary for growth and profitability.

Budgeting

Budgeting involves creating a detailed plan that forecasts the dispensary's revenues, expenses, and cash flows over a specific period, typically a year. This plan serves as a financial roadmap, guiding the dispensary in its financial decision-making process.

Start-Up Costs: Begin with a comprehensive estimate of start-up costs, including licensing fees, property lease or purchase, renovations, initial inventory purchases, equipment, and marketing expenses. Understanding these initial costs is crucial for securing adequate funding and setting the stage for operational planning.

Operational Expenses: Regular operational expenses, such as salaries, utilities, inventory restocking, marketing, and compliance costs, must be carefully forecasted. It's essential to account for the cyclical nature of some expenses, like higher inventory purchases to meet increased demand during certain periods.

Revenue Projections: Accurate revenue projections are challenging but crucial. These should be based on market research, considering factors like local demand, competition, and pricing strategies. Regularly updating these projections as the dispensary operates is vital for adapting to market changes.

Cash Flow Management: Given the cash-intensive nature of the cannabis industry, a detailed cash flow projection is essential. This should highlight when cash shortfalls might occur and plan for maintaining adequate liquidity to cover operational needs.

Financial Management

Effective financial management involves closely monitoring and controlling financial activities to ensure the dispensary operates within its means and meets its financial objectives.

-Accounting and Record-Keeping: Implement robust accounting practices to track revenues, expenses, and profits accurately. Given the complexities of cannabis taxation and compliance, consider using accounting software tailored to the cannabis industry or hiring professionals with relevant experience.

-Cost Control: Regularly review operational expenses to identify areas where costs can be reduced or controlled without compromising product quality or customer service. This might involve negotiating better terms with suppliers or investing in energy-efficient equipment.

- **Pricing Strategy:** Develop a dynamic pricing strategy that considers market demand, competition, and cost structures. Pricing strategies may include discounts, loyalty programs, or premium pricing for specialty products.

- **Tax Planning and Compliance:** Engage in proactive tax planning to navigate the complexities of cannabis taxation, particularly in jurisdictions like the United States, where Section 280E of the IRS code restricts business deductions. Understanding tax obligations and planning accordingly can significantly affect net profitability.

- **Investment in Growth:** Allocate a portion of the budget towards growth opportunities, such as expanding product lines, investing in marketing, or exploring new market areas. Careful financial planning is required to balance investment in growth with maintaining operational stability.

- **Financial Analysis and Review:** Regularly review financial statements and performance metrics to assess the dispensary's financial health and make informed decisions. This includes analyzing profitability, operating margins, and cash flow patterns.

- **Emergency Fund:** Establish an emergency fund to cover unexpected expenses or downturns in business. This fund provides a financial cushion that can help the dispensary navigate unforeseen challenges without compromising its operations or financial stability.

Effective budgeting and financial management require continuous attention and adaptation to changing market conditions, regulatory environments, and business needs. By prioritizing these practices, a medical marijuana dispensary can enhance its financial stability, support sustainable growth, and navigate the complexities of the cannabis industry with greater confidence.

Banking and Financial Services for Marijuana Businesses

Banking and financial services for marijuana businesses present a complex and evolving challenge due to the intersection of state-level legalization and federal prohibition in countries like the United States. Despite the legal status of medical and recreational marijuana in numerous states, marijuana remains classified as a Schedule I controlled substance under federal law. This classification significantly impacts the willingness and ability of federally regulated banks and financial institutions to offer services to marijuana-related businesses (MRBs), leading to a range of financial and operational challenges.

Challenges Faced by Marijuana Businesses

Limited Banking Access: Many banks, being federally regulated, are hesitant to provide services to MRBs due to the fear of federal enforcement action, even in states where marijuana is legal. This reluctance forces many marijuana businesses to operate primarily in cash, increasing the risks of theft, fraud, and operational inefficiencies.

Compliance and Reporting Requirements: Banks that choose to serve MRBs must comply with stringent reporting requirements set forth by the Financial Crimes Enforcement Network (FinCEN). These requirements include filing Suspicious Activity Reports (SARs) for transactions associated with marijuana businesses, which adds to the administrative burden and costs for banks.

Lack of Financing Options: The reluctance of traditional banks to engage with MRBs extends to financing. Many marijuana businesses find it challenging to secure loans, credit lines, or other financing options through conventional channels, limiting their ability to expand, invest in equipment, or manage cash flow effectively.

Emerging Solutions and Alternatives

Despite these challenges, some progress has been made in developing banking and financial services solutions for marijuana businesses:

State-Chartered Banks and Credit Unions: In some states with legal marijuana markets, state-chartered banks and credit unions have begun to offer banking services to MRBs, operating under state regulations and with a willingness to comply with the FinCEN guidelines. These institutions provide a range of services, including checking accounts, payroll services, and sometimes even loans.

Cash Management Solutions: Recognizing the risks associated with operating primarily in cash, some businesses offer specialized cash management services to MRBs. These services can include secure cash transport, counting, and storage, as well as assistance with paying taxes and vendors electronically, reducing the need to handle large amounts of cash.

Payment Processing Alternatives: To mitigate the reliance on cash, some MRBs have explored alternative payment methods, such as cryptocurrency, digital wallets, and block-chain technology. However, these solutions have their limitations and regulatory uncertainties.

Private Lenders and Investment Firms: Marijuana businesses often turn to private lenders, angel investors, and cannabis-focused investment firms for financing. While these sources can provide capital, they may come with higher interest rates or require giving up a degree of ownership or control.

Advocacy for Banking Reform: There is ongoing advocacy and legislative efforts aimed at reforming banking laws to allow financial institutions to serve state-legal marijuana businesses without fear of federal penalties. Legislation such as the SAFE Banking Act has been proposed to address these issues, although it has yet to be passed into law.

For marijuana businesses, navigating the banking and financial landscape requires a deep understanding of the regulatory environment, a commitment to compliance, and creativity in seeking alternative solutions. As the legal landscape evolves and societal attitudes towards marijuana continue to shift, there is hope for more accessible and comprehensive financial services for MRBs in the future.

Location Selection and Leasing

Selecting the right location and securing a lease are pivotal steps in establishing a medical marijuana dispensary. The chosen location not only affects the dispensary's accessibility to its target market but also its compliance with local zoning laws and regulations, which can significantly impact the business's operational feasibility and success.

Considerations for Location Selection

Compliance with State and Local Regulations: Most jurisdictions have specific zoning laws that restrict where dispensaries can operate. These often include requirements that dispensaries be a certain distance from schools, parks, daycares, and sometimes from other dispensaries. Before settling on a location, it's crucial to understand these regulations thoroughly to ensure compliance and avoid costly legal challenges.

Market Accessibility: The location should be easily accessible to the target market. Consider factors like visibility from major roads, convenience for patients in terms of parking and public transportation access, and the overall safety of the area. A location that's easy to access can enhance customer experience and contribute to higher foot traffic.

Demographic Compatibility: Understanding the demographics of the area is essential. The location should align with the demographic profile of the dispensary's target market. Areas with a higher prevalence of the conditions that medical marijuana can help manage might be more lucrative.

Competition Analysis: Proximity to competitors can have a significant impact on a dispensary's success. While being too close to another dispensary could saturate the market, being located in an area with little to no competition can offer a significant advantage. However, understanding why competitors are absent from an area is also important – it could be due to low demand or restrictive local regulations.

Securing a Lease

Once a suitable location is identified, negotiating and securing a lease requires careful attention to detail and an understanding of the unique aspects of leasing property for a dispensary.

Negotiation: Given the legal complexities surrounding dispensaries, landlords may be hesitant or demand higher rents due to perceived risks. It's important to negotiate terms that are favorable but realistic, considering these unique market dynamics. Having legal counsel with experience in the cannabis industry can be beneficial during these negotiations.

Lease Terms: The lease should clearly state the permitted use of the property as a dispensary to avoid future disputes. Additionally, clauses regarding compliance with state and local laws, and provisions for modifications or enhancements required for security and operations, should be explicitly covered.

Contingencies: Including contingency clauses in the lease that allow for termination of the agreement should state or local regulations change adversely can protect the business from unforeseen legal shifts. Similarly, securing options to renew can protect the dispensary from sudden lease terminations once the business is established.

Due Diligence: Before signing a lease, conducting thorough due diligence on the property is crucial. This includes verifying zoning laws, understanding any restrictions on property use, and ensuring that the property can be modified to meet the specific needs of a dispensary, including security requirements and patient privacy considerations.

Selecting the right location and successfully negotiating a lease are foundational steps in launching a medical marijuana dispensary. These decisions require a strategic approach, detailed market research, and often, the guidance of professionals experienced in real estate, legal, and cannabis industry specifics. With the right location, a dispensary can ensure compliance, attract and retain customers, and set the stage for successful operations.

Zoning and location criteria

Zoning and location criteria play a critical role in the establishment and operation of medical marijuana dispensaries. These regulations and considerations are designed to ensure dispensaries operate in appropriate areas while addressing community standards and safety concerns. Understanding and adhering to zoning laws and selecting a suitable location are pivotal steps in the licensing process and for the long-term success of a dispensary.

Zoning Laws

Zoning laws dictate how land within a municipality can be used, dividing areas into zones that specify allowable uses such as residential, commercial, industrial, and agricultural. For medical marijuana dispensaries, local governments have established specific zoning regulations that must be closely followed.

Proximity Restrictions: One of the most common zoning restrictions for dispensaries involves their proximity to schools, parks, daycares, and other dispensaries. These regulations are meant to minimize potential exposure to children and to avoid concentration in certain areas, which can vary significantly between jurisdictions.

Allowed Zones: Dispensaries are often restricted to certain zones, typically commercial or industrial areas, to align with local business and land use policies. It's crucial to verify that a prospective location is zoned for a dispensary before proceeding with lease negotiations or planning.

Local Approval: Some localities require dispensaries to obtain special permits or go through a conditional use permit process, which may involve public hearings and meeting additional criteria beyond basic zoning compliance. This process allows local governments to have more control over where and how dispensaries operate within their jurisdiction.

Location Criteria

Beyond zoning, several other criteria are essential when selecting a location for a medical marijuana dispensary. These considerations are crucial for accessibility, customer convenience, and operational efficiency.

Visibility and Access: A location with good visibility from major roads and easy access for customers, including ample parking and public transportation options, can enhance foot traffic and patient accessibility.

Security Considerations: Given the security requirements for dispensaries, including surveillance and secure product storage, locations need to accommodate these needs. An area perceived as safe by customers and where security measures can be effectively implemented is preferable.

Demographic Match: Understanding the demographics of the area and ensuring they align with the target market for medical marijuana is crucial. Areas with higher populations of patients who may benefit from medical marijuana are more likely to support a successful dispensary.

Market Saturation: Assessing the competitive landscape is important. While being close to competitors can signal a viable market, too much competition may limit growth potential. Identifying underserved areas can offer strategic advantages.

Future Growth: Consideration for future expansion possibilities can also influence location choice. A site that allows for physical expansion or has additional space for inventory can accommodate growing patient demand over time.

Navigating Zoning and Location Criteria

Successfully navigating zoning and location criteria requires thorough research, due diligence, and often the assistance of professionals such as real estate agents, lawyers, and consultants who specialize in the cannabis industry. They can provide invaluable insights into local regulations, assist in the site selection process, and help ensure compliance with all necessary legal and regulatory requirements.

Understanding and adhering to these zoning laws and location criteria not only facilitates the licensing and setup process but also positions a medical marijuana dispensary for operational success, ensuring it meets both legal requirements and patient needs effectively.

Negotiating leases for dispensary spaces

Negotiating leases for dispensary spaces is a nuanced process that requires careful consideration of the unique aspects of the cannabis industry, local regulations, and the specifics of the commercial real estate market. Successful lease negotiations can set the foundation for a prosperous operation, ensuring the dispensary is situated in an optimal location with terms that accommodate its specific needs. Here are key strategies and considerations for negotiating leases for dispensary spaces:

Understand Local Zoning and Regulations

Before entering negotiations, it's crucial to thoroughly understand the local zoning laws and regulations governing the placement of dispensaries. This knowledge will help narrow down viable locations and prevent wasting time on properties that cannot legally house a dispensary. It also positions you as an informed tenant, potentially strengthening your negotiating stance.

Assess the Property's Suitability

Evaluate the property's suitability for a dispensary operation, considering factors such as visibility, accessibility, customer parking, and proximity to complementary businesses. Security is also a paramount concern, so assess the ease of implementing necessary security measures, including surveillance cameras, secure product storage, and safe customer access.

Leverage a Real Estate Agent with Cannabis Experience

Working with a real estate agent experienced in the cannabis industry can provide valuable insights and advocacy during lease negotiations. These professionals understand the market dynamics, legal considerations, and typical lease terms for dispensaries, which can be leveraged to secure a favorable deal.

Negotiate Lease Terms Specific to Dispensaries

Given the unique aspects of operating a dispensary, including the potential for regulatory changes, it's important to negotiate lease terms that offer flexibility and protection. Consider including clauses that address:

Compliance Adjustments: The lease should allow for modifications to the premises to ensure ongoing compliance with cannabis regulations, which may change over time.

Early Termination Options: Due to the uncertain regulatory environment, negotiating an early termination clause can protect your business if it becomes impossible to operate due to legal changes.

Renewal Options: Secure the option to renew your lease under predetermined terms to avoid displacement at the end of your lease term, which can be crucial for maintaining customer base and operational continuity.

Addressing Landlord Concerns

Landlords may have concerns about leasing to cannabis businesses due to perceived legal risks, potential property damage, or increased insurance costs. Be prepared to address these concerns directly, offering reassurances such as:

Compliance Commitment: Emphasize your commitment to regulatory compliance, including adherence to all local, state, and federal laws.

Security Measures: Outline the security measures you'll implement to safeguard the property, products, and customers.

Insurance: Confirm that you will obtain adequate insurance to cover potential liabilities, reassuring the landlord of your proactive risk management approach.

Financial Terms

Due to the perceived risks and the limited pool of properties suitable for dispensaries, landlords may demand higher rents or more substantial security deposits.

Prepare to negotiate these financial terms by:

Market Research: Conduct thorough market research to understand typical lease rates and terms for similar commercial spaces in the area, using this data to inform your negotiations.

Financial Guarantees: Be ready to provide financial statements or guarantees to reassure the landlord of your business's stability and your ability to meet lease obligations.

Legal Review

Before finalizing any lease agreement, have it reviewed by an attorney experienced in real estate and cannabis law. This ensures that the lease terms protect your interests, comply with all relevant regulations, and provide a solid foundation for your dispensary's operations.

Negotiating leases for dispensary spaces requires a strategic approach that accounts for the unique challenges of the cannabis industry. By thoroughly understanding regulations, carefully evaluating potential spaces, addressing landlord concerns, and securing flexible and protective lease terms, dispensary operators can establish a strong foundation for their business's success.

Designing Your Dispensary for Success

Designing your dispensary for success involves more than just aesthetic appeal; it's about creating a space that is welcoming, functional, and compliant with regulatory requirements. A well-designed dispensary can enhance customer experience, streamline operations, and contribute to the overall success and sustainability of the business.

Here are key considerations and strategies for designing a successful medical marijuana dispensary:

Focus on Customer Experience

Welcoming Environment: Create a space that feels welcoming and safe for all customers, including those new to medical marijuana. Use warm lighting, comfortable seating, and inviting colors to make the space feel accessible and friendly.

Educational Spaces: Incorporate areas where customers can learn about different strains, products, and their medical benefits. Interactive displays, digital screens, or dedicated consultation rooms can facilitate education and informed decision-making.

Privacy Considerations: Design the layout to offer privacy for customers who may wish to discuss their medical conditions or treatment plans discreetly. Private consultation areas can help in providing personalized customer service.

Ensure Operational Efficiency

Streamlined Layout: Organize the dispensary layout to support efficient workflow and customer movement. Separate entrance and exit paths, clearly defined product areas, and an intuitive layout can reduce congestion and enhance the shopping experience.

Point of Sale (POS) Stations: Designate specific areas for sales transactions that are equipped with the necessary technology and security measures. Ensure these areas can accommodate peak traffic times without compromising customer service or privacy.

Back-of-House Functionality: Allocate space for back-of-house operations, including product storage, staff areas, and administrative offices. Consider the operational flow and security requirements when designing these spaces.

Prioritize Security

Visibility: Ensure that the design allows for clear visibility throughout the dispensary, both for staff to monitor the sales floor and for security cameras to cover all areas effectively.

Secure Product Displays: Use secure, locked display cases for product presentation, allowing customers to view products without direct access. This helps in maintaining inventory control and complying with security regulations.

Access Control: Implement security measures such as access control systems for entry into the dispensary and restricted areas. These systems can help in monitoring and controlling access, enhancing overall security.

Comply with Regulations

Accessibility: Ensure the dispensary design complies with the Americans with Disabilities Act (ADA) and other relevant accessibility standards, providing easy access for all customers.

Compliance with State Regulations: Design the dispensary to meet all state and local regulations related to security, storage, and operations. This may include specific requirements for product storage, surveillance systems, and secure transport areas.

Incorporate Branding

Consistent Branding: Use your dispensary's design to reinforce your brand identity. Incorporate your brand colors, logos, and themes throughout the interior and exterior design to create a memorable and cohesive brand experience.

Atmospheric Branding: Beyond visual elements, consider how other aspects of the design, such as lighting, music, and scent, can convey your brand's ethos and create a unique atmosphere that aligns with your brand identity. Designing your dispensary for success requires a holistic approach that considers customer experience, operational efficiency, security, regulatory compliance, and branding. By carefully planning and executing your dispensary's design, you can create a space that not only meets the practical needs of the business but also offers a welcoming, engaging, and memorable experience for your customers.

Licensing and Compliance

Licensing and compliance are foundational elements for operating a medical marijuana dispensary, ensuring that the business adheres to state and local regulations governing the sale of cannabis for medical purposes. Navigating the licensing process and maintaining ongoing compliance requires a thorough understanding of the regulatory landscape, meticulous attention to detail, and proactive management practices.

Here's an overview of the key aspects involved in licensing and compliance for a medical marijuana dispensary.

Licensing Process

The process for obtaining a license to operate a medical marijuana dispensary varies by jurisdiction but generally involves several critical steps:

Application Preparation: The initial step requires gathering and preparing extensive documentation, including business plans, financial statements, operational plans, and security protocols.

This phase may also require background checks for owners and key employees, as well as proof of a suitable location that complies with zoning requirements.

Submission and Fees: Once the application package is complete, it must be submitted along with the required non-refundable application fees. These fees can be significant, so it's essential to ensure that all application components meet the regulatory standards to avoid rejection.

Review Process: After submission, the application undergoes a review process by the regulatory authority. This phase may include inspections of the proposed location, interviews with the applicants, and a thorough review of the application materials to ensure compliance with state and local regulations.

Approval and Licensing Fees: If the application is approved, the dispensary will be required to pay the licensing fees before receiving the official license to operate. These fees can vary widely depending on the jurisdiction.

Renewals: Dispensary licenses typically have a validity period after which they must be renewed. The renewal process may require submitting updated documentation and undergoing additional inspections to ensure ongoing compliance.

Compliance Considerations

Once licensed, dispensaries must adhere to a comprehensive set of regulatory requirements to maintain their license and operate legally. Key areas of compliance include:

Product Tracking and Inventory Control: Most states require seed-to-sale tracking of all cannabis products to prevent diversion and ensure product safety. Dispensaries must use approved systems to track inventory accurately and report to the state regulatory body.

Security Measures: Dispensaries are required to implement robust security measures, including surveillance systems, secure storage for cannabis products, and access controls. These measures are designed to protect against theft, ensure patient safety, and comply with state regulations.

Patient Verification and Record-Keeping: Dispensaries must verify the eligibility of patients by checking medical marijuana cards and maintaining confidential records of transactions. Compliance with patient privacy laws and accurate record-keeping is essential for regulatory audits.

Product Testing and Labeling: State regulations often require that cannabis products be tested for potency and contaminants. Dispensaries must ensure that all products are accurately labeled with test results, dosage information, and consumption warnings.

Zoning and Local Ordinances: In addition to state regulations, dispensaries must comply with local ordinances, which may include specific zoning requirements, business hour restrictions, and community engagement standards.

Taxes and Financial Reporting: Cannabis businesses face unique tax liabilities and reporting requirements. Understanding and complying with these financial obligations, including federal tax code 280E, is crucial for legal and financial stability.

Maintaining compliance in the highly regulated cannabis industry requires ongoing vigilance, investment in compliance infrastructure, and a commitment to operational excellence. Dispensaries can benefit from engaging legal and compliance experts specializing in cannabis regulations to navigate the complexities of licensing and compliance, avoid costly penalties, and ensure the long-term success of the business.

Navigating the Licensing Process

Navigating the licensing process for a medical marijuana dispensary is a comprehensive and detailed endeavor that requires careful planning, adherence to regulations, and often, patience. Each state or country with legalized medical marijuana has its own set of rules and procedures, making it crucial for entrepreneurs to thoroughly understand the specific requirements of their jurisdiction.

Here's a general framework for navigating the licensing process, highlighting key steps and considerations:

1. Research and Understanding Regulations

The first step involves in-depth research to understand the specific licensing requirements, application process, fees, and regulatory landscape of the jurisdiction where the dispensary will operate. This includes:

- **State and local cannabis laws and regulations.**

- **Application deadlines, fees, and required documentation.**

- **Zoning and location restrictions for dispensaries.**

- **Operational, security, and compliance standards.**

2. Business Planning

Developing a comprehensive business plan is essential not only for the licensing application but also for the overall success of the dispensary. **The business plan should address:**

- The business model and value proposition.

- Detailed market analysis and target customer demographics.

- Product offerings and sourcing strategies.

- Operational workflow, including security and compliance measures.

- Financial projections and funding strategies.

- Ownership structure and management team qualifications.

3. Securing a Suitable Location

Finding a location that complies with zoning laws and is strategically positioned for business success is critical. This involves:

- Identifying zones where dispensaries are allowed to operate.

- Considering proximity to target customers and competitors.

- Ensuring the location is suitable for necessary security and operational modifications.

4. Gathering Required Documentation

The licensing application typically requires a multitude of documents, including:

- Owner and employee background checks.

- Financial statements and proof of funding.

- Detailed operational plans covering security, inventory tracking, and patient verification systems.

- Floor plans and property lease agreements or ownership documents.

- Community impact statements or plans.

5. Application Submission

With all necessary documentation and plans in place, the next step is to submit the licensing application along with the required fees. This step may also involve:

- Pre-application meetings or consultations with regulatory bodies.

- Submission of digital and physical application packets, as required.

6. Preparation for Inspection and Interviews

After submitting the application, be prepared for on-site inspections of the proposed location and interviews with the business owners and key staff members. This stage assesses the readiness and compliance of the dispensary with regulatory standards.

7. Application Review and Approval

The licensing authority will review the application, conduct necessary inspections and interviews, and make a decision. This process can take several months, depending on the jurisdiction and the complexity of the application.

8. License Issuance and Annual Renewals

If approved, the dispensary will receive its license to operate, often accompanied by specific conditions or restrictions. Dispensary owners must:

- Pay any final licensing fees.

- Adhere to all operational, security, and compliance requirements.

- Prepare for regular inspections and compliance checks.

- **Apply for license renewals as required, typically on an annual basis.**

9. Continuous Compliance

Maintaining compliance with state and local regulations is an ongoing responsibility. Dispensaries must stay informed of any changes in cannabis laws and regulations and adjust their operations accordingly.

Navigating the licensing process for a medical marijuana dispensary is a challenging but manageable journey with meticulous preparation, attention to regulatory details, and a commitment to operational excellence. Engaging with legal and consulting professionals who specialize in cannabis law and business practices can provide invaluable assistance throughout this process, helping to avoid common pitfalls and enhance the likelihood of success.

Compliance with State and Local Regulations

Compliance with state and local regulations is a cornerstone of operating a medical marijuana dispensary successfully. Given the complex and often fluctuating regulatory environment surrounding cannabis, dispensaries must navigate a labyrinth of laws that govern every aspect of their operation, from licensing, product sourcing, and sales to security measures and patient privacy. This compliance not only ensures the legal operation of the dispensary but also protects patients and aligns with community standards.

The foundation of compliance begins with understanding the specific regulatory requirements set forth by the state and local jurisdiction in which the dispensary operates. These laws cover a wide range of topics and can vary significantly from one location to another, reflecting local values, concerns, and experiences with medical marijuana. Regulations typically address the licensing process, including the application requirements, fees, and the criteria used to evaluate applicants. They also outline operational standards for dispensaries, specifying how cannabis products must be stored, tracked, and sold to ensure product integrity and patient safety.

Zoning laws are a critical aspect of compliance, dictating where dispensaries can be located within a community. These laws are designed to keep dispensaries away from schools, parks, and other areas frequented by minors, while also considering the impact on local businesses and residential areas. Compliance with zoning laws requires careful site selection and often involves engaging with local planning departments and community members to address any concerns and ensure the dispensary is a positive addition to the community.

Product testing and labeling requirements are another crucial component of regulatory compliance. States have established standards for testing cannabis products for potency and contaminants to ensure patient safety. Dispensaries must work with licensed testing facilities to verify that all products meet these standards before they are sold. Additionally, accurate labeling is required to provide patients with essential information about the product, including THC and CBD content, dosage recommendations, and potential side effects.

Security regulations are designed to prevent theft, diversion of cannabis products, and ensure the safety of dispensary staff and patients. Compliance in this area involves implementing robust security systems, including surveillance cameras, secure storage for cannabis products, and procedures for handling cash and product transfers. These measures are not only regulatory requirements but also critical for building trust with patients and the community. Record-keeping and reporting are essential for compliance and regulatory oversight. Dispensaries are required to maintain detailed records of their inventory, sales transactions, and patient information. Many states require dispensaries to use seed-to-sale tracking systems that monitor cannabis products from cultivation to sale, ensuring transparency and accountability in the supply chain. Accurate and timely reporting to state regulators allows for effective monitoring of the dispensary's operations and compliance status.

Compliance with state and local regulations is an ongoing process that requires dispensaries to stay informed about changes in the legal landscape. This may involve regularly reviewing regulatory updates, participating in industry associations, and engaging with legal and compliance experts who specialize in cannabis law. Training staff on compliance procedures and the importance of adherence to regulations is also critical for maintaining a culture of compliance within the dispensary.

Compliance with state and local regulations is a multifaceted and dynamic aspect of operating a medical marijuana dispensary. It encompasses a broad range of requirements, from licensing and zoning to product safety, security, and record-keeping. By prioritizing compliance, dispensaries can ensure their operations are legal, protect patient safety, and contribute positively to their communities. Given the evolving nature of cannabis laws, dispensaries must remain adaptable, informed, and proactive in their compliance efforts to navigate the complexities of the regulatory environment successfully.

Record-Keeping and Reporting Requirements

In the realm of medical marijuana dispensaries, meticulous record-keeping and reporting are not just operational necessities; they are integral to compliance with state and local regulations. The intricate web of laws governing the cannabis industry places a high emphasis on transparency, accountability, and the ability to trace products from seed to sale. As such, dispensaries must establish and maintain robust systems for documenting all aspects of their operation, from inventory management and financial transactions to patient interactions and compliance efforts.

At the heart of record-keeping requirements is the mandate to track the movement and sale of cannabis products accurately. This involves maintaining detailed logs of inventory purchases, storage, and sales, ensuring that each product can be traced back to its source.

This level of traceability is crucial for several reasons: it helps prevent the diversion of cannabis to the black market, ensures products are not contaminated or counterfeit, and facilitates recalls if safety issues arise. Many states require the use of specific seed-to-sale tracking systems that integrate with state regulatory databases, providing regulators with real-time access to inventory data.

Beyond inventory tracking, dispensaries must also keep comprehensive financial records. This includes sales receipts, banking transactions, payroll records, and tax documents. The unique legal status of cannabis at the federal level, particularly in the United States, complicates tax reporting and compliance, making accurate financial documentation even more critical. Dispensaries often operate in a predominantly cash-based economy due to restrictions on banking access, necessitating rigorous cash handling and documentation procedures to prevent theft and ensure accurate reporting.

Patient records are another critical aspect of a dispensary's record-keeping obligations. Dispensaries must document patient registrations, product purchases, and any adverse reactions reported, all while maintaining strict confidentiality in accordance with patient privacy laws. This information not only supports compliance with regulations limiting the amount of cannabis a patient can purchase but also enhances patient safety and the quality of care by allowing dispensaries to track patient preferences and reactions to specific strains or products.

Reporting requirements typically involve submitting regular summaries of inventory, sales, and compliance activities to state and local regulators. These reports may be required monthly, quarterly, or annually, depending on the jurisdiction, and are essential for maintaining the dispensary's license to operate. Failure to submit accurate and timely reports can result in fines, suspension of operations, or revocation of the dispensary's license.

To meet these extensive record-keeping and reporting requirements, dispensaries must invest in reliable information technology systems and train staff on proper documentation practices. This often involves implementing specialized dispensary management software that can handle seed-to-sale tracking, financial accounting, and patient management in a compliant and efficient manner. Regular audits of record-keeping systems, both internal and by third-party compliance experts, can help identify and correct potential issues before they result in regulatory violations.

Effective record-keeping and reporting are fundamental to the operation of medical marijuana dispensaries, underpinning their ability to comply with regulatory requirements, maintain financial integrity, and ensure patient safety. By establishing robust systems for documenting inventory, financial transactions, and patient interactions, dispensaries can navigate the complexities of the cannabis regulatory environment, maintain their license to operate, and build trust with regulators, patients, and the community.

Product Acquisition and Inventory Management

Product acquisition and inventory management are critical components in the operation of a medical marijuana dispensary, ensuring that a wide range of high-quality cannabis products is available to meet patient needs while maintaining compliance with regulatory requirements. Effective management in these areas involves careful selection of suppliers, rigorous product testing, accurate tracking, and strategic stock management. These processes are not only essential for operational efficiency and customer satisfaction but also for adhering to the strict regulatory environment of the cannabis industry.

Product Acquisition

The process of acquiring products for a dispensary involves several key steps, starting with identifying reputable suppliers who can provide a consistent supply of high-quality cannabis products. This includes cultivators, processors, and manufacturers of various cannabis forms, such as flowers, concentrates, edibles, tinctures, and topicals. Dispensaries must conduct due diligence on potential suppliers to ensure they adhere to cultivation and production standards, use safe and sustainable practices, and comply with state regulations regarding product testing for potency and contaminants.

Building strong relationships with suppliers is crucial for ensuring product quality and reliability. Dispensaries may negotiate contracts that specify delivery schedules, pricing, and quality standards, providing a stable supply chain that can adapt to changing inventory needs and market demands. In jurisdictions where vertical integration is allowed or required, dispensaries may also engage in cultivating and processing their own products, which adds an additional layer of management in terms of production planning, compliance, and quality control.

Inventory Management

Once products are acquired, effective inventory management becomes essential to ensure that the dispensary operates efficiently, meets patient demand, and complies with regulatory requirements for product tracking and reporting. Key aspects of inventory management include:

Stock Levels: Maintaining optimal stock levels is crucial to prevent overstocking, which can lead to product degradation or financial loss, or understocking, which can result in missed sales opportunities. Dispensaries use sales data and trend analysis to forecast demand and adjust inventory levels accordingly.

Product Diversity: Offering a diverse product range caters to varying patient preferences and medical needs. Inventory management strategies must balance the demand for popular strains and products with the desire to introduce new and diverse offerings to keep the product lineup fresh and engaging.

Seed-to-Sale Tracking: Most states require dispensaries to implement seed-to-sale tracking systems that monitor cannabis products throughout the supply chain. These systems track the movement and sale of each product, ensuring compliance with regulatory requirements for traceability and preventing diversion to the illicit market.

Storage and Security: Proper storage of cannabis products is essential to maintain their quality and potency. Dispensaries must implement secure storage solutions that control temperature, humidity, and light exposure, in addition to security measures that prevent theft and unauthorized access.

Compliance and Reporting: Inventory management systems must facilitate compliance with state regulations, including accurate record-keeping and reporting of inventory levels, sales, and product disposals. Regular audits and reconciliation of physical inventory with recorded data help ensure accuracy and compliance.

Effective product acquisition and inventory management require a combination of strategic planning, technological tools, and operational best practices. By focusing on supplier relationships, product diversity, efficient stock management, and regulatory compliance, dispensaries can ensure a steady supply of high-quality cannabis products that meet patient needs and contribute to the dispensary's success.

Establishing Relationships with Growers and Suppliers

Establishing relationships with growers and suppliers is a critical aspect of running a successful medical marijuana dispensary. Strong partnerships ensure a consistent supply of high-quality products that meet the needs and preferences of patients. These relationships are built on trust, reliability, and mutual understanding of the cannabis industry's regulatory environment.

Here's an in-depth look at how dispensaries can establish and maintain effective relationships with growers and suppliers.

Understanding the Supply Chain

The first step in establishing relationships is to understand the cannabis supply chain thoroughly. This involves knowing the journey of cannabis products from seed to sale, including cultivation, harvesting, processing, and distribution. Dispensaries should familiarize themselves with the various types of suppliers in the market, from small-scale artisanal growers specializing in unique strains to large-scale cultivators and manufacturers that produce a wide range of cannabis products.

Due Diligence and Selection Criteria

Choosing the right growers and suppliers involves comprehensive due diligence. Dispensaries should evaluate potential partners based on several criteria, including:

Quality of Products: Assess the quality of the cannabis strains and products offered. This includes potency, purity, and consistency of products, as well as compliance with safety and testing standards.

Cultivation Practices: Prefer growers who use sustainable and ethical cultivation practices. This might include organic farming methods, responsible water usage, and avoidance of harmful pesticides.

Regulatory Compliance: Ensure that growers and suppliers are fully compliant with state and local regulations. This includes proper licensing, adherence to testing requirements, and transparent labeling practices.

Reliability and Scalability: Evaluate the supplier's ability to provide consistent product quality and quantities. Assess their capacity to scale up supply in response to growing demand.

Pricing and Terms: Negotiate fair pricing and favorable terms that benefit both parties. Consider the long-term value of the relationship beyond just the cost of goods.

Building Relationships

Once suitable growers and suppliers have been identified, the focus shifts to building and nurturing these relationships. Key strategies include:

Communication: Maintain open and frequent communication with suppliers. Regular updates, feedback, and discussions about market trends can help align business strategies and expectations.

Collaboration: Work collaboratively with growers and suppliers to develop exclusive strains or products that can differentiate your dispensary in the market. Collaborative projects can strengthen partnerships and provide mutual benefits.

Long-Term Agreements: Consider establishing long-term contracts that offer stability and security for both the dispensary and the supplier. This can lead to better pricing, priority supply, and a strong commitment from both parties.

Flexibility and Understanding: Be understanding and flexible in dealing with challenges that may arise, such as crop failures or regulatory changes. A supportive approach can foster loyalty and trust in the relationship.

Monitoring Performance and Ensuring Compliance

Continuous monitoring of supplier performance and compliance is crucial for maintaining successful relationships. Regularly review product quality, delivery times, and adherence to contractual terms. Conduct periodic audits or site visits to verify cultivation practices and compliance with regulatory standards.

Cultivating a Network

Beyond individual relationships with growers and suppliers, dispensaries should also cultivate a broader network within the cannabis industry. This can include participation in industry associations, trade shows, and conferences, which provide opportunities to meet new suppliers, stay informed about industry developments, and share best practices.

Establishing and maintaining strong relationships with growers and suppliers is essential for the success of a medical marijuana dispensary. These partnerships ensure a reliable supply of high-quality cannabis products, enabling dispensaries to meet patient needs effectively while navigating the complexities of the cannabis industry.

Choosing product assortments

Choosing the right product assortments for a medical marijuana dispensary involves a delicate balance between meeting patient needs, staying compliant with regulations, and navigating market trends. The assortment of products offered can significantly impact the dispensary's ability to attract and retain customers, influence its reputation, and ultimately, its financial success. Here's a closer look at the strategic considerations involved in selecting product assortments.

Understanding Patient Needs: The cornerstone of any successful dispensary is its ability to meet the diverse needs of its patients. This involves offering a range of products that cater to different medical conditions, preferences, and consumption methods. Engaging with patients through surveys, feedback, and one-on-one interactions can provide valuable insights into their needs and preferences. Products can include various strains of cannabis flowers, edibles, concentrates, topicals, tinctures, and CBD products, each with different THC and CBD concentrations to cater to different therapeutic needs.

Staying Informed on Regulations: Regulatory compliance is non-negotiable when selecting product assortments. Dispensaries must be well-versed in state and local regulations governing the sale of medical marijuana, including restrictions on certain types of products, packaging, labeling, and potency limits. Staying informed and compliant not only protects the dispensary from legal penalties but also ensures the safety and trust of its patients.

Monitoring Market Trends: The cannabis industry is rapidly evolving, with new products and consumption methods continually emerging. Keeping a finger on the pulse of industry trends allows dispensaries to stay competitive and innovative. This might involve introducing new strains, CBD products, or alternative consumption methods such as vape pens, patches, or dissolvable strips. However, while it's important to offer trendy products, dispensaries should also ensure these items meet the same high standards for quality and safety as their core offerings.

Curating a Quality Selection: Quality should never be compromised when choosing product assortments. Dispensaries should establish stringent criteria for selecting suppliers, focusing on product purity, consistency, and safety. This often involves requiring third-party lab testing results for contaminants and potency, visiting cultivation or production facilities, and assessing the supplier's reputation and reliability. Offering high-quality products not only benefits patients but also enhances the dispensary's reputation and patient loyalty.

Diversifying Product Offerings: Diversification is key to catering to a broad patient base. This includes not only offering a variety of product types and strains but also considering factors such as potency, price points, and brand offerings. A well-diversified product assortment can attract a wider range of patients, from those new to medical marijuana looking for low-potency or non-intoxicating options to experienced patients seeking specific strains or higher-potency products.

Educational Support and Staff Training: Choosing product assortments also involves ensuring that dispensary staff are knowledgeable and can provide educational support to patients. Staff should be trained on the details of each product, including its intended use, dosage recommendations, and potential side effects. This educational approach can help patients make informed decisions and feel more confident in their purchases.

Inventory Management: Effective inventory management goes hand in hand with choosing product assortments. Dispensaries need to balance supply with demand, avoiding overstocking on slow-moving products while ensuring popular items are always in stock. This involves regular review of sales data, patient feedback, and inventory levels, adjusting product orders accordingly to optimize stock levels and meet patient demand.

Choosing the right product assortments for a medical marijuana dispensary is a complex process that requires a deep understanding of patient needs, regulatory compliance, market trends, and quality assurance. By carefully curating their product offerings, dispensaries can meet the diverse needs of their patients, build trust, and position themselves for long-term success in the competitive medical marijuana market.

Inventory Management Practices

Inventory management in a medical marijuana dispensary is a complex task that requires precision, regulatory compliance, and strategic planning. The goal is to ensure that the dispensary maintains an optimal assortment of products to meet patient needs while minimizing waste, avoiding stock-outs, and ensuring compliance with state and local regulations.

Effective inventory management practices in this context involve several key strategies and tools:

Regular Inventory Audits

Conducting regular inventory audits is critical for maintaining accurate records and ensuring compliance with regulatory requirements. Physical counts should be compared against inventory records to identify discrepancies and adjust records as needed. These audits help in identifying trends such as fast-moving products, slow sellers, or potential issues with theft or diversion.

Seed-to-Sale Tracking Systems

Utilizing seed-to-sale tracking systems is mandated in many jurisdictions to ensure regulatory compliance and product traceability. These systems track cannabis products from cultivation through to the final sale to patients, providing real-time inventory data. Implementing such systems helps dispensaries monitor stock levels, manage reordering, and report inventory accurately to regulatory bodies.

Data-Driven Inventory Decisions

Leveraging sales data and analytics can inform inventory management decisions, helping dispensaries forecast demand, identify trends, and adjust product assortments accordingly. Analyzing sales data allows dispensaries to optimize their product mix, focusing on high-demand products while reducing or eliminating slow-moving inventory.

Supplier Relationships

Maintaining strong relationships with suppliers is vital for effective inventory management. Open communication about stock levels, delivery timelines, and product quality can help dispensaries manage their inventory more effectively. Building partnerships with reliable suppliers ensures a consistent supply of products, reducing the risk of stock-outs.

Diverse Product Assortment

Offering a diverse product assortment is important for meeting the varied needs and preferences of patients. Dispensaries should regularly review their product mix, considering patient feedback, market trends, and regulatory changes. However, it's also crucial to balance diversity with inventory control, avoiding overextension that can lead to excessive carrying costs or product obsolescence.

Strategic Ordering and Stocking

Implementing strategic ordering practices, such as just-in-time (JIT) inventory or economic order quantity (EOQ) models, can help dispensaries minimize excess inventory and reduce storage costs. Careful planning of reorder points and quantities ensures that dispensaries maintain enough stock to meet patient demand without tying up too much capital in inventory.

Loss Prevention Strategies

Developing and enforcing loss prevention strategies is crucial for minimizing shrinkage due to theft, diversion, or spoilage. This includes secure storage practices, employee training on proper handling and tracking of products, and security measures to deter and detect theft.

Compliance and Record-Keeping

Adhering to compliance requirements and maintaining meticulous records are non-negotiable aspects of inventory management in the cannabis industry. Dispensaries must ensure that all inventory practices meet state and local regulations, including product testing, packaging, labeling, and reporting. Keeping detailed records supports regulatory compliance, audit readiness, and operational transparency.

Effective inventory management in a medical marijuana dispensary requires a combination of technological tools, data analytics, strategic planning, and compliance adherence. By implementing these practices, dispensaries can optimize their inventory levels, meet patient needs effectively, and operate successfully within the regulatory framework of the cannabis industry.

Staffing Your Dispensary

Staffing your medical marijuana dispensary involves more than just filling positions; it's about building a team that is knowledgeable, trustworthy, and aligned with your dispensary's mission and values. The staff plays a crucial role in the overall patient experience, compliance with regulations, and the operational success of the dispensary. Therefore, thoughtful consideration and strategic planning are essential in recruiting, training, and retaining the right team members.

Recruitment

Start by identifying the key roles required to operate your dispensary effectively. Common positions include budtenders, dispensary managers, security personnel, inventory specialists, and customer service representatives. For each role, develop detailed job descriptions that outline responsibilities, required qualifications, and desired attributes. This clarity helps attract candidates who are a good fit for both the position and your dispensary's culture.

Recruitment strategies should be diverse and targeted. Utilize online job boards, especially those specific to the cannabis industry, social media platforms, and networking events. Employee referrals can also be a valuable source of candidates, as current employees are likely to recommend individuals who fit well with your dispensary's culture and values.

Selection Process

The selection process should be thorough and structured to assess candidates' knowledge, skills, and fit with your dispensary's culture. In addition to traditional interviews, consider incorporating role-specific assessments, such as product knowledge tests for budtenders or customer service scenarios for front-of-house staff. It's also essential to conduct background checks to ensure the trustworthiness and reliability of potential employees, especially given the compliance and security requirements of the cannabis industry.

Training

Comprehensive training is critical for ensuring that your staff is equipped to provide high-quality patient care, comply with regulations, and maintain operational standards. Training programs should cover:

- Cannabis knowledge, including the effects of different strains, consumption methods, and medical benefits.

- Compliance and legal requirements, focusing on state and local cannabis regulations, patient verification processes, and inventory tracking.

- Customer service skills, emphasizing empathy, communication, and discretion to provide a supportive and informative patient experience.

- Operational procedures, such as point-of-sale systems, inventory management, and security protocols.

Ongoing training and professional development opportunities can help staff stay informed about industry developments, enhance their skills, and feel valued and engaged in their roles.

Retention

Retaining skilled and motivated staff is as important as recruiting them. Competitive compensation, benefits, and a positive work environment are fundamental to retention. Additionally, creating opportunities for career advancement and recognizing and rewarding outstanding performance can foster loyalty and commitment among your team.

Encouraging open communication and feedback, involving staff in decision-making processes, and building a supportive team culture can also enhance job satisfaction and reduce turnover. Regular team meetings and feedback sessions allow employees to share ideas, address concerns, and feel connected to your dispensary's mission and success.

Staffing your medical marijuana dispensary is a strategic process that requires careful planning and ongoing effort. By attracting the right candidates, providing comprehensive training, and fostering a positive and engaging work environment, you can build a dedicated team that contributes to the exceptional care of your patients, compliance with regulations, and the overall success of your dispensary.

Hiring Qualified Staff

Hiring qualified staff for a medical marijuana dispensary is a critical step toward ensuring the success and sustainability of the business. The unique nature of the cannabis industry, coupled with its regulatory complexities, demands a workforce that is not only skilled and knowledgeable but also adaptable and committed to compliance and exceptional customer service.

Here's a detailed approach to hiring qualified staff for a dispensary:

Define Clear Job Roles and Qualifications

Start by clearly defining the roles and responsibilities for each position within the dispensary. This clarity helps in identifying the specific skills, knowledge, and attributes needed for each role. For example, budtenders should possess an in-depth understanding of cannabis products and their effects, strong communication skills, and a compassionate approach to customer service. Managers, on the other hand, need experience in retail management, regulatory compliance, and team leadership.

Utilize Targeted Recruitment Strategies

Recruitment strategies should be tailored to attract candidates with the right mix of experience, knowledge, and cultural fit. Utilize industry-specific job boards, social media platforms, and professional networks to reach a targeted audience. Participation in cannabis industry events and job fairs can also be effective in attracting talent. Additionally, consider leveraging your dispensary's website and social media channels to showcase your workplace culture and values, attracting candidates who align with your mission.

Implement a Rigorous Selection Process

The selection process should be designed to thoroughly assess candidates' qualifications, experience, and fit for the role. This can include:

Initial Screening: Review resumes and cover letters to identify candidates who meet the essential qualifications.

Interviews: Conduct structured interviews that explore candidates' knowledge of cannabis, customer service experience, and scenarios that assess their problem-solving and ethical decision-making skills.

Skill Assessments: Depending on the role, consider including practical assessments, such as product knowledge quizzes for budtenders or inventory management exercises for inventory specialists.

Background Checks: Given the regulatory environment of the cannabis industry, comprehensive background checks are essential to ensure candidates' eligibility to work in the sector and their adherence to legal and compliance standards.

Focus on Training and Development

Once hired, providing comprehensive training to new staff members is crucial for equipping them with the knowledge and skills necessary to perform their roles effectively. Training programs should cover product knowledge, regulatory compliance, customer service best practices, and operational procedures. Ongoing training opportunities can also support staff development and adaptability to changes within the industry and regulatory landscape.

Foster a Positive Work Environment

Creating a supportive and inclusive work environment is key to retaining qualified staff. This includes offering competitive compensation and benefits, opportunities for career advancement, and a workplace culture that values teamwork, communication, and mutual respect. Encouraging feedback and open dialogue can also help in identifying and addressing any issues or concerns, contributing to job satisfaction and employee engagement.

Hiring qualified staff for a medical marijuana dispensary requires a thoughtful and structured approach, from clear role definitions and targeted recruitment to rigorous selection processes and comprehensive training. By investing in the recruitment and development of a skilled and dedicated team, dispensaries can ensure high-quality customer service, compliance with regulatory requirements, and the overall success of their operation.

Training and Education for Employees

Training and education for employees in a medical marijuana dispensary are pivotal for ensuring the staff is knowledgeable, compliant with regulations, and equipped to provide exceptional service to patients. Given the complexities of the cannabis industry and the critical role dispensaries play in patient care, comprehensive training programs are essential. These programs cover a range of topics, from cannabis science and product knowledge to regulatory compliance and customer service excellence.

A well-structured training program begins with an orientation that introduces new employees to the dispensary's mission, values, and operational procedures. This initial phase sets the stage for a deeper understanding of the dispensary's culture and expectations.

It's also an opportunity to familiarize employees with the legal landscape of the cannabis industry, emphasizing the importance of compliance in every aspect of the operation.

Core to the training program is an in-depth exploration of cannabis science, including the plant's anatomy, cannabinoids, terpenes, and the endocannabinoid system. This knowledge base enables employees to understand how cannabis interacts with the body and the potential therapeutic benefits of different strains and product formulations. Employees learn to navigate the variety of consumption methods, from inhalation and ingestion to topical application, and the implications of each method for onset time, duration of effects, and dosing considerations.

Product knowledge training is equally critical, as employees must be able to advise patients on the selection of products that best meet their medical needs and preferences. This includes understanding the nuances of different strains, potency levels, and product quality. Training should also cover the proper storage and handling of cannabis products to maintain their efficacy and safety.

Regulatory compliance is a cornerstone of the training program. Employees must be well-versed in state and local cannabis laws, including patient verification processes, purchase limits, and record-keeping requirements.

Training in this area ensures that employees can confidently navigate the regulatory environment, reducing the risk of violations that could jeopardize the dispensary's license and reputation.

Customer service training focuses on developing the skills needed to provide a supportive, respectful, and informative experience for patients. Employees learn to communicate effectively, listen actively, and handle sensitive topics with discretion. Training in conflict resolution and de-escalation techniques is also important, preparing employees to manage challenging interactions professionally.

Given the dynamic nature of the cannabis industry, ongoing education and training are crucial. This can include regular updates on regulatory changes, new product offerings, and advances in cannabis research. Encouraging employees to participate in external training programs, conferences, and seminars can also broaden their knowledge and skills, fostering professional growth and development.

Effective training and education for dispensary employees are not just about transferring knowledge; it's about building a team that is passionate, empathetic, and committed to patient care. By investing in comprehensive training programs, dispensaries can enhance the quality of service, ensure operational compliance, and contribute to the overall success of the business.

This commitment to employee development reflects the dispensary's dedication to excellence and its role in promoting health and wellness through cannabis.

Staff Management and Retention Strategies

Staff management and retention strategies in a medical marijuana dispensary are essential for maintaining a knowledgeable, motivated, and cohesive team. In the rapidly evolving cannabis industry, dispensaries face unique challenges in staffing, including navigating regulatory complexities and addressing the stigma associated with cannabis. Effective staff management and retention strategies help dispensaries overcome these challenges, fostering a positive work environment and ensuring long-term success.

Creating a Positive Workplace Culture

A positive workplace culture is foundational for staff retention. This involves building an environment where employees feel valued, respected, and part of a team. Encouraging open communication, fostering inclusivity, and promoting a sense of community among staff can enhance job satisfaction and loyalty. Celebrating successes, acknowledging individual and team achievements, and facilitating social interactions outside of work can strengthen bonds among employees.

Competitive Compensation and Benefits

Offering competitive compensation and benefits packages is crucial for attracting and retaining top talent. This includes not only fair wages but also health insurance, retirement savings plans, paid time off, and other perks such as employee discounts on products. Regularly reviewing and adjusting compensation packages to reflect industry standards and the cost of living can help ensure that dispensaries remain attractive employers.

Professional Development and Career Advancement

Investing in professional development opportunities demonstrates a commitment to employees' growth and career advancement. This can include sponsoring attendance at industry conferences, providing access to training programs, and supporting continuing education. Establishing clear career paths and promoting from within whenever possible can motivate employees to invest in their roles and aspire to advance within the organization.

Flexible Scheduling and Work-Life Balance

Recognizing the importance of work-life balance and offering flexible scheduling options can significantly impact staff retention. Flexibility might include accommodating school schedules, providing opportunities for remote work when possible, or offering compressed workweeks. Understanding and addressing the personal needs of employees can lead to greater job satisfaction and reduce burnout.

Regular Feedback and Performance Evaluations

Implementing a structured system for providing regular feedback and conducting performance evaluations helps employees understand their contributions and areas for improvement. Constructive feedback and recognition of accomplishments can enhance morale and performance. Engaging employees in setting their goals and discussing career aspirations can also contribute to a more motivated workforce.

Involvement in Decision-Making

Involving employees in decision-making processes, especially those that directly affect their work or the dispensary environment, can foster a sense of ownership and engagement. Soliciting feedback on operational improvements, product selections, and customer service strategies can provide valuable insights and demonstrate that employee opinions are valued.

Addressing Employee Concerns Promptly

Promptly addressing concerns and grievances is critical for maintaining trust and respect. Establishing clear procedures for reporting and resolving workplace issues ensures that employees feel heard and supported. Proactively addressing potential sources of dissatisfaction can prevent minor grievances from escalating into reasons for leaving.

Building a Supportive Management Team

Training managers to be effective leaders who support, motivate, and guide their teams is essential for staff retention. Managers should be accessible, empathetic, and skilled in conflict resolution. They play a key role in implementing retention strategies, fostering a positive work environment, and ensuring that employees feel supported in their roles.

Effective staff management and retention strategies are crucial for the success of a medical marijuana dispensary. By creating a positive workplace culture, offering competitive compensation and benefits, investing in professional development, and fostering open communication, dispensaries can retain a committed and high-performing team. These strategies not only enhance the dispensary's operational effectiveness but also contribute to a superior patient experience.

Security Measures

Security measures in a medical marijuana dispensary are of paramount importance, not just for compliance with stringent regulatory requirements but also for ensuring the safety of employees, patients, and the community. Given the value of cannabis products and the cash-intensive nature of the industry, dispensaries are potential targets for theft and burglary. Additionally, the regulatory landscape mandates comprehensive security protocols to prevent diversion and ensure product integrity. Implementing robust security measures involves a multifaceted approach that encompasses physical security, operational procedures, technology, and employee training.

At the core of dispensary security is a well-designed physical security infrastructure. This includes secure, reinforced entry points to control access to the dispensary. Advanced locking systems, such as biometric locks or card access systems, can provide an additional layer of security. Windows should be fortified with security film or bars, and the perimeter of the property may be secured with fencing, particularly in standalone locations. Lighting plays a critical role in deterring unauthorized access or vandalism, with bright, strategically placed lighting around the building's exterior and parking areas enhancing visibility and safety.

Surveillance systems are indispensable for dispensary security. High-resolution cameras should cover all areas of the dispensary, including sales floors, storage areas, entry and exit points, and parking lots. These systems should allow for remote monitoring and have sufficient storage capacity to retain footage for a period specified by local regulations, often 30 days or more. Integration of surveillance with alarm systems can provide real-time alerts of any unauthorized access attempts, allowing for swift response.

Access control within the dispensary ensures that only authorized personnel can enter certain areas, particularly where cannabis products are stored or where sensitive information is kept. This not only helps prevent theft but also ensures compliance with regulations requiring that cannabis products be stored securely. Inventory should be stored in safes or secure cabinets, with access logged and monitored to track product movement and prevent diversion.

Operational procedures are vital for reinforcing physical security measures. This includes protocols for opening and closing the dispensary, handling cash, receiving deliveries, and responding to security incidents. Cash management procedures are particularly important, given the risks associated with handling and storing large amounts of cash.

Strategies might include the use of drop safes, regular bank deposits by secure transport, and minimal cash handling in customer-facing areas.

Employee training is a cornerstone of effective security. Staff should be trained on all security procedures, including how to identify and respond to security threats, proper cash handling practices, and emergency response protocols. Regular security drills can help ensure that employees are prepared to act decisively and appropriately in the event of an incident.

Technology also plays a role in enhancing security. In addition to surveillance and access control systems, dispensaries can employ inventory tracking technologies that provide real-time monitoring of product movement, further preventing diversion. Cybersecurity measures are equally important to protect patient information, financial data, and compliance records from cyber threats.

Collaboration with local law enforcement can enhance dispensary security. Establishing a good relationship with local police and sharing security plans can facilitate a quicker response in the event of an incident and contribute to overall community safety.

Security measures in a medical marijuana dispensary require a comprehensive strategy that integrates physical security infrastructure, operational protocols, technology, and employee training. By prioritizing security, dispensaries can protect their assets, ensure regulatory compliance, and provide a safe environment for employees and patients alike.

Physical security requirements

Physical security requirements for a medical marijuana dispensary are designed to safeguard the premises, protect assets, ensure the safety of employees and patients, and comply with state and local regulations. These requirements often involve a combination of structural fortifications, surveillance systems, access control measures, and specific operational protocols that collectively create a secure environment for conducting business. Implementing these requirements necessitates careful planning and investment in security infrastructure.

Structural Security Measures

The physical structure of the dispensary must be fortified to deter unauthorized access and prevent break-ins. This includes solid exterior walls, secure roofing, and tamper-resistant doors and windows. Entry points should be equipped with high-quality locks, and windows may need security bars or shatter-resistant film to provide additional protection. The layout of the dispensary should be designed to minimize vulnerabilities, with a clear line of sight from the sales floor to the entrance and strategically placed barriers to control customer flow.

Surveillance Systems

State-of-the-art video surveillance is a cornerstone of dispensary security, providing continuous monitoring of the interior and exterior of the premises. Cameras should be positioned to cover all critical areas, including point-of-sale stations, product display areas, storage rooms, and parking lots. Surveillance systems must offer high-resolution imaging, night vision capabilities, and sufficient storage capacity to retain footage for a period specified by regulations, often 30 to 90 days. Remote access to live and recorded footage enhances the ability to monitor the dispensary outside of business hours.

Access Control

Access control systems regulate entry to the dispensary and specific areas within it, such as inventory storage rooms. These systems can range from keypads and card readers to more sophisticated biometric systems that recognize fingerprints or retinal patterns. Access should be restricted based on employee roles, with a log of entries and exits to track access to sensitive areas. This not only enhances security but also aids in compliance by ensuring that only authorized personnel handle or have access to cannabis products.

Alarm Systems

Comprehensive alarm systems are required to detect unauthorized access or attempted break-ins. These systems should be connected to doors, windows, and possibly motion detectors to alert local law enforcement and dispensary management in the event of a security breach. Panic buttons can also be strategically placed to allow employees to quickly signal for help in case of an emergency.

Secure Product Storage

Cannabis products and cash are high-value items that require secure storage. Regulations often dictate that these items be stored in safes or reinforced vaults that are bolted to the structure of the building. The location of these storage solutions should be discreet, with access controlled and monitored through the dispensary's access control system.

Operational Security Measures

Beyond physical infrastructure, dispensaries must implement operational security measures. This includes protocols for opening and closing the dispensary, handling deliveries, managing cash, and responding to security incidents. Employees should be trained to follow these protocols diligently, ensuring consistent application of security practices.

Compliance with Regulations

Finally, dispensaries must ensure that all physical security measures comply with state and local regulations, which can vary widely. Regulatory bodies may require dispensaries to submit security plans for approval before issuing a license, and ongoing compliance may be monitored through inspections. Failure to meet these requirements can result in fines, revocation of the dispensary's license, or other penalties.

Physical security requirements for a medical marijuana dispensary are multifaceted, involving a combination of structural enhancements, technology, controlled access, and operational protocols. By adhering to these requirements, dispensaries can protect against theft, ensure the safety of employees and patients, and maintain compliance with regulatory standards, supporting the long-term success and sustainability of the business.

Security Protocols and Procedures

Security protocols and procedures in a medical marijuana dispensary are designed to protect the premises, products, employees, and customers. These protocols encompass a range of practices from physical security measures to operational routines and emergency responses, ensuring compliance with regulatory standards and promoting a safe environment. Implementing and adhering to these protocols is vital for the dispensary's integrity and reputation.

Employee Training and Awareness

A foundational aspect of effective security protocols is comprehensive employee training. Employees should be educated on all aspects of security, from the operation of surveillance and alarm systems to the procedures for handling suspicious behavior or emergency situations. Regular training sessions help maintain a high level of security awareness among staff and ensure that everyone understands their role in maintaining a safe dispensary.

Access Control

Controlling access to the dispensary and sensitive areas within it is critical. Access control protocols might involve electronic key cards, biometric scanners, or PIN codes, ensuring that only authorized personnel can enter certain parts of the building, especially where cannabis products or cash are stored. Logs of who enters and exits secure areas should be maintained to track access and identify potential security breaches.

Surveillance Monitoring

Continuous monitoring of surveillance feeds is a key security protocol. Cameras should cover all angles of the dispensary, including entry and exit points, sales floors, and storage areas. Security personnel or designated staff members should regularly review footage to detect any unusual activities or discrepancies. Modern surveillance systems allow for remote monitoring, which can enhance security oversight outside of business hours.

Cash Handling Procedures

Given the cash-intensive nature of the cannabis industry, dispensaries must implement strict cash handling procedures. This includes using safes for storing large amounts of cash, making regular bank deposits, and employing discreet methods for transferring cash between the dispensary and financial institutions.

Employees should receive training on minimizing cash exposure and ensuring transactions are conducted securely.

Emergency Response Plans

Dispensaries should have detailed emergency response plans in place for various scenarios, including robberies, medical emergencies, fires, and natural disasters. These plans should outline the steps employees must take in response to different emergencies, including contacting law enforcement or emergency services, securing the premises, and ensuring the safety of customers and staff. Regular drills can help familiarize staff with these procedures and ensure a calm and coordinated response in actual emergency situations.

Product Handling and Inventory Control

Protocols for handling cannabis products and managing inventory are essential for security and regulatory compliance. This includes procedures for receiving deliveries, storing products securely, conducting inventory audits, and disposing of waste or unsold products. Seed-to-sale tracking systems can assist in monitoring product movement and ensuring that inventory levels match sales records.

Incident Reporting and Documentation

A clear protocol for reporting and documenting security incidents or breaches is necessary. This includes maintaining logs of all incidents, no matter how minor, and reporting significant security breaches to law enforcement and regulatory agencies as required. Documentation supports investigations, regulatory compliance, and continuous improvement of security measures.

Regular Security Reviews

Finally, dispensaries should conduct regular reviews of their security protocols and procedures. This involves assessing the effectiveness of current measures, identifying vulnerabilities, and making necessary adjustments. Staying informed about new security technologies and evolving regulatory requirements can also inform these reviews and help dispensaries enhance their security practices over time.

Implementing and regularly updating security protocols and procedures are crucial for the safe and compliant operation of a medical marijuana dispensary. These practices not only protect the dispensary's assets and stakeholders but also contribute to the trust and confidence of customers and the community.

Compliance with Security Regulations

Compliance with security regulations in the medical marijuana industry is a critical component of operating a dispensary. These regulations are designed to safeguard the product from seed to sale, protect employees and customers, prevent theft or diversion, and ensure that operations align with both state and local laws. Given the varied and often strict regulatory landscape across different jurisdictions, dispensaries must meticulously adhere to a range of security requirements to maintain their licenses and operate legally.

Understanding Regulatory Requirements

The first step in ensuring compliance with security regulations is to thoroughly understand the specific requirements set by state and local authorities. These can include:

- Mandatory security systems, including surveillance cameras with specific resolution and storage capacity requirements, alarm systems, and access control measures to restrict entry to authorized personnel.

- Protocols for the secure transportation of cannabis products from cultivation sites to the dispensary and, in some cases, from the dispensary to the customer in the case of delivery services.

- Specifications for the secure storage of cannabis products and cash on the premises, often requiring safes or vaults that meet certain security standards.

- Record-keeping requirements for tracking product movement and sales transactions, often necessitating the use of state-approved seed-to-sale tracking systems.

Implementing Security Measures

Once the regulatory requirements are understood, dispensaries must implement the necessary security measures. This often involves investing in high-quality surveillance equipment, installing secure display cases and storage solutions, and adopting electronic inventory tracking systems. Dispensaries may also need to design their physical layout to enhance security, such as creating a single, secure entry point for customers and separate, locked areas for product storage.

Training and Policies

Ensuring that all employees are trained on security policies and procedures is crucial for compliance. This training should cover the proper use of security systems, emergency response procedures, cash handling protocols, and product tracking. Employees should also be educated on the legal requirements for verifying customer eligibility and maintaining patient privacy. Regular training updates can help ensure that staff remains informed about any changes in regulatory requirements or security best practices.

Regular Audits and Compliance Checks

To maintain ongoing compliance with security regulations, dispensaries should conduct regular audits of their security measures and practices. This can involve reviewing surveillance footage to ensure cameras are functioning correctly, testing alarm systems, verifying that access controls are in place and effective, and checking inventory records against physical stock to prevent diversion. These audits can help identify any areas of non-compliance or security vulnerabilities that need to be addressed.

Engagement with Regulatory Agencies

Proactive engagement with regulatory agencies can also support compliance efforts. This may include seeking clarification on security requirements, reporting security incidents as required, and submitting to regular inspections by state or local authorities. Building a positive relationship with regulatory agencies can facilitate a more collaborative approach to compliance and help ensure that the dispensary remains in good standing.

Adapting to Changes

Dispensaries must be prepared to adapt to changes in security regulations. The cannabis industry is evolving rapidly, and regulatory requirements can change as new legislation is enacted or as authorities update policies based on industry developments. Staying informed about potential regulatory changes and being proactive in updating security measures and practices are essential for ensuring long-term compliance.

Compliance with security regulations is a complex but essential aspect of operating a medical marijuana dispensary. By thoroughly understanding regulatory requirements, implementing robust security measures, training employees, conducting regular audits, engaging with regulatory agencies, and staying adaptable to changes, dispensaries can ensure the safety and security of their operations while meeting legal obligations.

Marketing and Customer Relations

Marketing and customer relations in the medical marijuana industry are pivotal for dispensaries aiming to distinguish themselves in a competitive market. Given the unique regulatory environment and the sensitive nature of the product, strategies in this domain must be both innovative and compliant, focusing on building trust and educating the target audience. A comprehensive approach to marketing and customer relations not only drives business growth but also contributes to destigmatizing medical cannabis, fostering a more informed and accepting community.

The foundation of effective marketing in the medical marijuana sector is a deep understanding of the target market. This involves recognizing the diverse needs and preferences of medical cannabis patients, who may range from individuals seeking relief from chronic pain, anxiety, or other conditions, to those exploring cannabis as an alternative to traditional medications. Tailoring marketing messages to address the specific concerns and interests of these groups, while always prioritizing education and empathy, can enhance engagement and loyalty.

Digital marketing plays a crucial role, given the restrictions often faced in traditional advertising channels. A well-designed website serves as the centerpiece of a dispensary's online presence, offering comprehensive information about products, usage methods, and the medical conditions they can help address. Content marketing, through blogs and educational resources, can position the dispensary as a trusted authority in medical cannabis. Social media platforms, while navigated carefully due to policy restrictions, offer opportunities for engagement, education, and community building. Email marketing campaigns can keep patients informed about new products, special promotions, and industry news, fostering a sense of connection and loyalty.

Local SEO strategies ensure that the dispensary appears prominently in search results when potential customers look for medical cannabis options in their area. This involves optimizing the website for relevant keywords, maintaining accurate and comprehensive listings in online directories, and encouraging satisfied patients to leave positive reviews.

Beyond digital marketing, community engagement initiatives can significantly enhance a dispensary's visibility and reputation. Participating in health fairs, sponsoring local events, or hosting educational seminars can demonstrate the dispensary's commitment to the community and patient education.

Collaborations with healthcare providers and advocacy groups can also broaden the dispensary's reach and credibility.

Customer relations are equally vital, with a focus on creating a welcoming, inclusive, and supportive environment for patients. This involves training staff to be knowledgeable about medical cannabis, patient, and compassionate in their interactions. Personalized consultations can help patients understand their options and make informed choices, enhancing their experience and satisfaction. Feedback mechanisms, such as surveys or suggestion boxes, allow dispensaries to gather insights into patient needs and preferences, driving continuous improvement.

Loyalty programs and patient appreciation events can further strengthen relationships, rewarding repeat business, and fostering a sense of community among patients. Clear and transparent communication, particularly regarding product availability, pricing, and regulatory compliance, builds trust and reliability.

In addressing marketing and customer relations, dispensaries must always navigate the regulatory landscape carefully, ensuring that all marketing materials and customer interactions comply with state and local laws. This includes avoiding unsubstantiated health claims, ensuring privacy and confidentiality, and adhering to any restrictions on advertising and patient engagement.

Marketing and customer relations in the medical marijuana industry require a thoughtful balance between innovative engagement strategies and strict adherence to regulatory requirements. By focusing on education, community engagement, and personalized patient care, dispensaries can build strong relationships, foster loyalty, and contribute positively to the broader acceptance and understanding of medical cannabis.

Building a brand for your dispensary

Building a brand for your medical marijuana dispensary involves creating a distinctive identity that resonates with your target audience, distinguishes you from competitors, and communicates your values and commitment to quality patient care. A strong brand not only helps in attracting and retaining patients but also plays a crucial role in navigating the competitive and regulatory landscape of the cannabis industry.

Here's an in-depth exploration of how to build a compelling brand for your dispensary:

Define Your Brand Identity

Start by defining your brand identity, which includes your mission, values, and the unique value proposition you offer to patients. Consider what sets your dispensary apart from others: Is it your extensive product selection, your focus on patient education, your commitment to sustainability, or your community involvement? Your brand identity should reflect the core of what your dispensary stands for and aims to achieve.

Know Your Audience

Understanding your target audience is essential for building a brand that speaks directly to their needs and preferences. Consider the demographics, medical conditions, lifestyle choices, and cannabis usage habits of your patients. This knowledge allows you to tailor your branding and marketing efforts to resonate with your audience, ensuring that your message is relevant and compelling.

Develop a Visual Identity

Your brand's visual identity includes your logo, color scheme, typography, and imagery, all of which should be consistently applied across all your marketing materials and digital platforms. A well-designed visual identity helps in creating a memorable impression and fosters brand recognition. Ensure that your visual branding is professional, appealing, and aligned with the overall tone and message you want to convey.

Craft a Compelling Message

Your brand message should encapsulate what your dispensary is about and what it promises to deliver to patients. This message should be clear, concise, and infused with your brand's personality, whether that's compassionate, professional, innovative, or community-focused. Your brand message will guide your content across various marketing channels, from your website and social media to advertising and in-store signage.

Leverage Digital Platforms

A strong online presence is crucial for building your dispensary's brand. This includes a user-friendly website that provides valuable information about your products, services, and the medical conditions they can help address. Social media platforms offer opportunities to engage with your audience, share educational content, and build a community around your brand. However, it's essential to navigate the policies of each platform regarding cannabis content carefully.

Focus on Patient Experience

The patient experience is a critical component of your brand. Every interaction, from the moment patients enter your dispensary to the follow-up communication, should reflect your brand's values and commitment to excellence. Training your staff to provide knowledgeable, friendly, and compassionate service is key to reinforcing your brand identity and building long-term patient loyalty.

Engage with the Community

Building a brand for your dispensary also involves engaging with the broader community and the cannabis industry. Participating in local events, supporting charitable causes, and collaborating with other businesses can enhance your brand's visibility and reputation. Establishing your dispensary as a positive force in the community and an advocate for the benefits of medical cannabis can differentiate your brand and attract supportive patients.

Building a brand for your medical marijuana dispensary is a multifaceted process that encompasses defining your identity, understanding your audience, developing a cohesive visual and messaging strategy, leveraging digital platforms, prioritizing patient experience, and engaging with the community. A strong brand not only helps in attracting and retaining patients but also contributes to the overall success and sustainability of your dispensary in the competitive cannabis market.

Marketing Strategies and Channels

In the competitive landscape of the medical marijuana industry, dispensaries must employ strategic marketing efforts to attract and retain patients while navigating the complex regulatory environment. Effective marketing strategies and channels are essential for building brand awareness, educating potential patients about the benefits of medical cannabis, and driving foot traffic to the dispensary. Given the restrictions on cannabis advertising in many jurisdictions, creativity and compliance are paramount in devising marketing plans.

One core strategy involves developing a strong online presence. This starts with a professional, user-friendly website that serves as the hub for your dispensary's online activities. The website should offer comprehensive information about your products, including detailed descriptions, usage methods, and potential benefits for various medical conditions. Including a blog or resource section with educational content can further establish your dispensary as a trusted authority in medical cannabis. SEO (Search Engine Optimization) practices are crucial for enhancing your website's visibility in search engine results, making it easier for potential patients to find you.

Social media marketing, despite its challenges due to platform restrictions on cannabis-related content, remains a powerful tool for engaging with your audience. Platforms like Instagram, Facebook, and Twitter can be used to share educational content, behind-the-scenes glimpses of your dispensary, and patient testimonials (with proper permissions). It's important to familiarize yourself with each platform's policies on cannabis to navigate these channels effectively without risking account suspension.

Email marketing campaigns can be an effective way to maintain communication with your patient base, offering personalized content such as product updates, promotional offers, and educational materials directly to their inboxes. Building a compliant email list requires patients to opt-in, ensuring they're interested in receiving communications from your dispensary.

Community engagement presents another valuable marketing avenue. Participating in local events, sponsoring health fairs, or offering educational seminars on medical cannabis can increase your visibility and credibility within the community. These activities not only promote your dispensary but also contribute to destigmatizing medical cannabis use.

Loyalty programs incentivize repeat visits and foster patient loyalty by rewarding them for their patronage. Such programs can include points systems, discounts on birthdays, or special access to limited-edition products. These incentives can encourage ongoing engagement and increase patient retention.

Collaborations with healthcare providers and patient advocacy groups can also serve as an effective marketing strategy. By establishing relationships with medical professionals and organizations, dispensaries can gain referrals and enhance their legitimacy in the eyes of potential patients.

It's also worth exploring traditional marketing channels, such as print advertising in local publications, radio spots, or outdoor advertising, where regulations permit. While digital marketing offers broad reach and targeting capabilities, traditional channels can complement online efforts, especially in reaching demographics less active on social media.

In developing marketing strategies and selecting channels, dispensaries must always consider the regulatory framework governing cannabis advertising. This often means avoiding claims about health benefits, ensuring content is targeted at an adult audience, and including disclaimers where required. Staying informed about changes in advertising regulations is crucial for maintaining compliance and protecting your dispensary from potential penalties.

Marketing strategies and channels for medical marijuana dispensaries require a blend of digital and community-focused efforts, grounded in educational content and patient engagement. By navigating regulatory challenges with creativity and compliance, dispensaries can effectively market their offerings, build strong patient relationships, and grow their presence in the medical cannabis industry.

Customer Service and Retention Strategies

In the competitive landscape of the medical marijuana industry, customer service and retention strategies are pivotal for dispensaries aiming to establish a loyal patient base and differentiate themselves. The emphasis on exceptional customer service stems from the understanding that patients seeking medical marijuana often have specific, sometimes critical, health needs, making the quality of service a significant factor in their dispensary choice. Retention strategies further build on this foundation, ensuring that once patients choose a dispensary, they have compelling reasons to remain loyal.

At the heart of effective customer service in a medical marijuana dispensary is a knowledgeable and empathetic staff. Employees should receive comprehensive training not just on the products offered but also on patient care and communication. Understanding the medical conditions that cannabis can help manage and being able to guide patients in choosing the right products for their needs is crucial. Empathy plays a key role, as many patients may be new to medical marijuana and require guidance and reassurance.

Personalization enhances the patient experience significantly. Tailoring service to individual patient needs, preferences, and their history with the dispensary can make patients feel valued and understood. This might include maintaining patient profiles that track purchase history and preferences, which can then inform recommendations and personalize communication.

Clear and transparent communication is another cornerstone of customer service. This involves providing patients with detailed information about products, including their effects, dosage, and proper usage, as well as being upfront about pricing, policies, and procedures. Educating patients about the medical marijuana program in their state, including legal rights and responsibilities, can also contribute to a positive dispensary experience.

Engagement beyond the point of sale fosters a deeper connection with patients. This can be achieved through follow-up contacts to inquire about product satisfaction, informative newsletters, and educational events. Social media platforms and blogs offer avenues to share valuable content, news, and updates, keeping the dispensary top of mind for patients.

Loyalty programs are a direct retention strategy, incentivizing repeat visits and purchases. These programs can offer points for purchases, discounts on frequent purchases, birthday bonuses, or access to exclusive events and products. Loyalty programs not only encourage continued patronage but also generate a sense of belonging among patients.

Requesting and acting on feedback demonstrates that a dispensary values its patients' opinions and is committed to continuous improvement. This can be facilitated through surveys, suggestion boxes, or direct conversations. Addressing feedback not only improves the service quality but also builds trust and loyalty by showing patients that their input can lead to real changes.

Community involvement further strengthens the bond between dispensaries and their patients. Participating in health fairs, sponsoring local events, or supporting local charities aligns the dispensary with the well-being of the community and can engender loyalty from patients who value community engagement.

Customer service and retention strategies in a medical marijuana dispensary revolve around creating a patient-centered experience that prioritizes knowledge, empathy, personalization, and engagement. By implementing these strategies, dispensaries can build strong relationships with their patients, fostering loyalty and ensuring long-term success in the competitive medical marijuana market.

Operational Management

Operational management in a medical marijuana dispensary encompasses the comprehensive oversight of daily activities to ensure efficiency, compliance, and exceptional patient service. Given the unique regulatory environment of the cannabis industry, dispensaries face distinct operational challenges, including product sourcing, inventory management, compliance with state and local regulations, and providing knowledgeable patient care. Effective operational management strategies are crucial for navigating these complexities and sustaining a successful dispensary.

Streamlining Workflow and Processes

Creating efficient workflows and processes is vital for the smooth operation of a dispensary. This includes everything from product intake and inventory management to patient check-in and sales transactions. Implementing a point-of-sale (POS) system designed for cannabis retail can streamline operations, automate sales reporting, and ensure compliance with tracking requirements. Clear protocols for each operational aspect minimize errors and delays, enhancing the overall patient experience.

Inventory Management

Effective inventory management is a cornerstone of operational management, ensuring that the dispensary maintains an optimal balance of products to meet patient needs without overstocking. Utilizing inventory management software allows dispensaries to track product levels in real-time, forecast demand based on historical sales data, and automate reordering processes. Regular inventory audits help maintain accuracy in stock levels and compliance with state regulations on product tracking and reporting.

Compliance and Legal Adherence

Compliance with state and local regulations is non-negotiable for dispensaries. Operational management must include ongoing education on regulatory changes, meticulous record-keeping, and ensuring all aspects of the operation, from product labeling and packaging to security measures and patient verification, meet legal standards. Employing a compliance officer or dedicating resources to compliance training and audits can safeguard the dispensary against violations and penalties.

Employee Training and Development

Investing in employee training and development is essential for maintaining a knowledgeable and motivated staff capable of delivering high-quality patient service. Training programs should cover cannabis product knowledge, regulatory compliance, customer service best practices, and emergency response procedures. Encouraging professional development and providing clear paths for career advancement can also enhance staff retention and satisfaction.

Financial Management

Sound financial management practices are critical for the dispensary's viability and growth. This includes budgeting, managing cash flow, navigating the complexities of cannabis taxation, and strategic pricing to remain competitive while ensuring profitability. Employing financial management software or consulting with professionals experienced in cannabis finance can provide dispensaries with the insights and tools needed to manage their finances effectively.

Customer Service and Patient Education

Operational management extends to fostering a positive environment for patients, characterized by respectful, informative, and personalized service. Dispensaries should prioritize patient education, offering resources and consultations to help patients make informed decisions about their cannabis treatment. Strategies for collecting and acting on patient feedback contribute to continuous improvement in service quality.

Utilizing Technology

Technology plays a pivotal role in operational management, offering solutions for enhancing efficiency, compliance, and patient engagement. In addition to POS and inventory management systems, dispensaries can leverage online platforms for patient education, appointment booking, and product reservations. Ensuring cybersecurity measures are in place to protect patient data and operational information is also a critical aspect of utilizing technology in dispensary operations.

Daily Operations and Workflow

Managing daily operations and workflow in a medical marijuana dispensary involves coordinating various tasks and processes to ensure efficient service delivery, compliance with regulations, and a positive customer experience. A well-structured daily workflow helps dispensaries manage the complexities of retail operations while adhering to the stringent regulatory environment of the cannabis industry. Here's a closer look at how dispensaries can optimize their daily operations and workflow:

Opening Procedures

The day begins with opening procedures that ensure the dispensary is ready to welcome patients. This typically includes:

- Security checks to ensure that the premises are secure and that surveillance systems are functioning correctly.

- Counting and verifying cash in registers to start the day's transactions.

- Reviewing inventory levels and updating display cases with products.

- Briefing staff on the day's priorities, any special promotions, or product highlights.

Patient Check-In and Consultation

As patients arrive, they are checked in, which may involve verifying their medical marijuana cards and entering their information into the dispensary's patient management system. For new patients, this process might include an introductory consultation to discuss their needs and provide information on the types of products that might be beneficial for their condition.

Sales and Customer Service

The core of daily operations involves assisting patients in selecting products, providing detailed information about product benefits, usage, and dosage, and processing sales transactions. Budtenders play a crucial role in this process, requiring in-depth knowledge of the dispensary's product offerings and excellent customer service skills to ensure patients feel informed and supported in their choices.

Inventory Management

Throughout the day, staff must manage inventory, which includes receiving new shipments, updating inventory records, and conducting spot checks to ensure accuracy. Effective inventory management is critical for compliance with seed-to-sale tracking requirements and for maintaining optimal stock levels to meet patient demand.

Compliance and Record-Keeping

Daily operations also involve meticulous record-keeping to ensure compliance with state and local regulations. This includes logging sales transactions, maintaining patient records, and documenting any product returns or disposals. Regular audits of these records help dispensaries identify any discrepancies and address them promptly.

Cleaning and Maintenance

Maintaining a clean and welcoming environment is essential for dispensaries. Daily cleaning tasks might include sanitizing high-touch areas, tidying product displays, and ensuring that consultation areas are clean and organized. Routine maintenance checks of equipment and facilities also help prevent any operational disruptions.

Closing Procedures

At the end of the day, dispensaries undertake closing procedures to secure the premises and prepare for the following day. This typically involves:

- Conducting a final inventory check and securing products in locked storage.

- Counting cash, reconciling sales, and preparing deposits.

- Running end-of-day reports to review sales performance and inventory levels.

- Setting security systems and ensuring the dispensary is securely locked.

Staff Debriefing

A brief staff meeting at the end of the day can provide an opportunity to discuss the day's operations, highlight any issues or successes, and plan for upcoming days. This fosters a team environment and ensures that all staff are aligned with the dispensary's operational goals.

Optimizing daily operations and workflow in a medical marijuana dispensary requires careful planning, coordination, and a commitment to regulatory compliance and customer service. By establishing clear procedures for each aspect of the operation and empowering staff with the training and tools they need, dispensaries can create an efficient, compliant, and patient-focused environment.

Quality Control and Product Safety

Quality control and product safety are paramount concerns in the medical marijuana industry, directly impacting patient health and the integrity of dispensaries. The cannabis market's regulatory environment mandates stringent quality control measures, reflecting the industry's shift towards ensuring that products are not only effective but also safe for consumption. Dispensaries, therefore, must adopt comprehensive approaches to guarantee the quality and safety of their products, from sourcing to sale.

The foundation of quality control in a dispensary starts with the careful selection of growers and suppliers. This involves vetting their cultivation and production practices to ensure they adhere to high standards. Preferred suppliers are those who implement organic farming practices, avoid harmful pesticides and chemicals, and consistently produce cannabis of high potency and purity. Establishing strong relationships with these suppliers allows dispensaries to have greater transparency and influence over the quality of products they procure.

Upon receiving products, dispensaries must conduct thorough inspections to verify their quality and safety. This may include visual inspections to check for mold, pests, or other contaminants, as well as reviewing certificates of analysis (COAs) provided by third-party labs that test for cannabinoid profiles, terpenes, and potential contaminants such as pesticides, heavy metals, and microbial impurities. Ensuring that products meet state-specific regulatory standards for safety and potency is crucial for compliance and patient trust.

Inventory management plays a critical role in maintaining product quality. Proper storage conditions, such as controlled temperatures and humidity levels, are essential to preserve the integrity of cannabis products, preventing degradation of cannabinoids and terpenes. Dispensaries must also implement first-in, first-out (FIFO) inventory practices to ensure that older products are sold before fresher stock, reducing the risk of selling expired or deteriorated products.

Education and training of dispensary staff are fundamental to upholding quality control and product safety standards. Employees must be knowledgeable about the products they sell, including how to handle and store them safely, and how to communicate usage and dosage information to patients accurately. This knowledge enables staff to identify and address potential quality issues before products reach the consumer and to advise patients on safe consumption practices.

To further ensure product safety, dispensaries can advocate for and participate in industry-wide efforts to establish standardized testing and labeling requirements. Consistent, transparent labeling that includes detailed cannabinoid profiles, terpene content, and clear warnings about potential side effects helps patients make informed decisions and use products safely.

Establishing a feedback loop with patients is invaluable for quality control. Encouraging patients to report their experiences, both positive and negative, with the products they purchase can provide dispensaries with real-time insights into product efficacy, potential adverse reactions, and overall patient satisfaction. This feedback can guide future product selections and quality improvement initiatives.

Quality control and product safety in the medical marijuana industry require a multi-faceted approach that encompasses vigilant supplier selection, rigorous product inspection, careful inventory management, staff education, and patient feedback. By prioritizing these aspects, dispensaries not only comply with regulatory requirements but also build trust with patients, ensuring they receive safe, effective, and high-quality cannabis products.

Handling Customer Feedback and Complaints

Handling customer feedback and complaints effectively is crucial for any business, including medical marijuana dispensaries, where trust and patient satisfaction are paramount. Given the personal nature of medical cannabis use and the varying needs and experiences of patients, dispensaries may encounter feedback and complaints ranging from product quality and effectiveness to service and operational concerns. Addressing these issues thoughtfully and proactively can strengthen patient relationships, enhance service quality, and contribute to the dispensary's reputation for excellence.

Active Listening and Empathy

The initial step in handling feedback and complaints is to listen actively and empathetically. Patients who reach out with feedback are often looking for acknowledgment of their concerns. Whether the feedback is positive or negative, showing that you genuinely care and understand their experience is vital. This approach not only helps in gathering valuable insights into the patient's issue but also diffuses tension and builds trust.

Immediate Acknowledgment

Respond promptly to feedback and complaints, acknowledging receipt and expressing gratitude for the patient's willingness to share their experience. This immediate acknowledgment assures the patient that their feedback is valued and that the dispensary is committed to addressing their concerns. It sets a positive tone for the resolution process.

Investigate and Analyze

Before responding in detail, take the time to investigate the complaint thoroughly. This may involve reviewing the patient's purchase history, consulting with staff members involved, and examining relevant operational or service processes. Understanding the root cause of the issue is essential for providing a meaningful resolution and for identifying opportunities for improvement.

Personalized Responses

Craft personalized responses to feedback and complaints, avoiding generic or templated replies. Personalization shows that you have considered the specific circumstances and concerns of the patient. When addressing complaints, explain the steps you have taken to investigate the issue, offer a sincere apology if appropriate, and propose a solution or compensation if warranted. For positive feedback, express appreciation and highlight any action taken in response, such as sharing compliments with staff or implementing suggested improvements.

Resolution and Follow-Up

Offer a fair and prompt resolution to complaints, aligning with the dispensary's policies and the patient's expectations when possible. Solutions might include refunds, exchanges, discounts on future purchases, or other gestures that demonstrate a commitment to patient satisfaction. After resolving the issue, follow up with the patient to ensure they are satisfied with the outcome and to reaffirm your commitment to high-quality service.

Leverage Feedback for Improvement

Beyond individual resolutions, aggregate and analyze feedback and complaints to identify trends, operational challenges, or training opportunities. This analysis can inform strategic improvements in products, services, and processes, enhancing overall patient experience and operational efficiency. Sharing how patient feedback has led to specific changes can also demonstrate responsiveness and a commitment to continuous improvement.

Train Staff in Feedback Management

Equipping staff with the skills and authority to address feedback and complaints effectively is crucial. Provide training on active listening, empathy, conflict resolution, and the dispensary's policies for handling different types of feedback. Empowered and knowledgeable staff can often resolve issues swiftly, enhancing patient trust and satisfaction.

Handling customer feedback and complaints in a medical marijuana dispensary requires a structured yet personalized approach that prioritizes active listening, prompt acknowledgment, thorough investigation, and meaningful resolution. By treating feedback as an opportunity for improvement and demonstrating a genuine commitment to patient satisfaction, dispensaries can foster trust, loyalty, and a positive reputation in the community.

Ethical Considerations and Community Engagement

Ethical considerations and community engagement are integral components of operating a medical marijuana dispensary, reflecting a commitment to responsible business practices, patient care, and social responsibility. As the medical marijuana industry continues to evolve, dispensaries find themselves navigating complex ethical terrain, balancing profitability with patient well-being, and addressing broader societal concerns related to cannabis use. Engaging with the community and upholding high ethical standards fosters trust, legitimacy, and a positive reputation, which are crucial for long-term success in this field.

Ethical considerations in a medical marijuana dispensary encompass various dimensions, including patient care, product integrity, and transparency. Prioritizing patient well-being involves more than just providing high-quality cannabis products; it also means ensuring that staff are well-trained to offer compassionate, informed guidance to patients navigating medical cannabis treatments. This includes being honest about the potential benefits and limitations of cannabis, respecting patient privacy, and avoiding the overselling or inappropriate recommendation of products.

Product integrity is another critical ethical concern, requiring dispensaries to rigorously verify the safety, quality, and sourcing of their cannabis products. This means partnering with reputable growers and producers who adhere to sustainable and ethical cultivation practices, ensuring products are free from harmful contaminants, and accurately labeling products to inform patients about cannabinoid content, dosage, and consumption methods. Ethical sourcing extends to ensuring that suppliers uphold labor rights and environmental standards, reflecting a broader commitment to social responsibility.

Transparency is vital in building trust with patients and the community. This involves clear communication about product sourcing, pricing, and business practices. Dispensaries should also be transparent about their compliance with regulatory requirements and their efforts to address any concerns or issues that arise. Openly sharing information about the dispensary's operations and impact demonstrates accountability and a commitment to ethical conduct.

Community engagement represents an extension of a dispensary's ethical commitment, offering a means to contribute positively to the local area and foster mutual respect and understanding. Engaging with the community can take various forms, from participating in local events and supporting charitable causes to offering educational programs about medical cannabis. These initiatives can help demystify cannabis, reduce stigma, and highlight the dispensary's role in improving patient quality of life.

Community engagement involves listening to and addressing community concerns about the presence and operation of a medical marijuana dispensary. This might include efforts to mitigate any negative perceptions, such as increased traffic or safety concerns, and demonstrating how the dispensary contributes to local economic development and public health.

Ethical considerations and community engagement are not static but require ongoing attention and adaptation as the industry and societal attitudes evolve. Dispensaries that proactively address these areas can navigate the complexities of the medical marijuana market with integrity and foster a loyal patient base and supportive community relationships.

Social Responsibility in The Cannabis Industry

Social responsibility in the cannabis industry encompasses a broad range of practices aimed at positively impacting society and the environment. As the industry continues to grow and evolve, businesses within this sector are uniquely positioned to address historical injustices associated with cannabis prohibition, promote sustainability, and contribute to community well-being. Social responsibility in the cannabis industry involves several key areas, including ethical business practices, environmental stewardship, community engagement, and advocacy for policy reform.

Ethical Business Practices

Social responsibility begins with ethical business operations. This includes ensuring fair labor practices, providing safe and inclusive work environments, and offering fair wages and benefits to employees. Ethical sourcing of products is also crucial, with a focus on transparency and sustainability in the supply chain. Businesses can prioritize partnerships with suppliers who adhere to organic farming practices, avoid harmful pesticides, and implement fair labor standards.

Environmental Stewardship

The cannabis industry faces significant environmental challenges, including water usage, energy consumption, and waste generation, particularly in cultivation and production processes. Socially responsible cannabis businesses are adopting sustainable practices to mitigate their environmental impact. This can involve using energy-efficient lighting and climate control systems in cultivation facilities, implementing water conservation techniques, and utilizing organic cultivation methods to reduce the reliance on chemical fertilizers and pesticides. Recycling programs and packaging made from sustainable or biodegradable materials also contribute to reducing the industry's environmental footprint.

Community Engagement and Support

Engaging with and supporting local communities is a central aspect of social responsibility in the cannabis industry. Dispensaries and other cannabis businesses can play a positive role in their communities by sponsoring local events, supporting charitable causes, and providing education about medical cannabis. Initiatives that focus on economic development, such as supporting local small businesses or creating job opportunities, can have a lasting positive impact. Additionally, many businesses are actively involved in supporting communities disproportionately affected by cannabis prohibition, offering support through education, job training, and expungement programs to help individuals with prior cannabis convictions rebuild their lives.

Advocacy for Policy Reform

Given the historical context of cannabis prohibition and its disproportionate impact on marginalized communities, advocacy for policy reform is a crucial component of social responsibility in the cannabis industry. Businesses and industry groups are increasingly involved in advocating for legal reforms that address social justice issues, such as expunging past cannabis convictions, ensuring equitable access to cannabis business licenses, and redirecting cannabis tax revenues to communities harmed by prohibition. Supporting policy changes that promote a fair, equitable, and inclusive industry is essential for correcting past injustices and ensuring that the benefits of legalization are shared broadly.

Education and Research

Promoting education and research is another important aspect of social responsibility. Dispensaries and cannabis companies can contribute to the wider understanding of cannabis by funding research into its medical benefits and potential risks, supporting educational initiatives that provide accurate information about cannabis use, and dispelling myths and misinformation. Education efforts can also focus on responsible consumption practices, helping to ensure that consumers are informed and safe.

Social responsibility in the cannabis industry is multifaceted, encompassing ethical operations, environmental sustainability, community engagement, advocacy for justice and policy reform, and support for education and research. As the industry continues to mature, embracing these principles of social responsibility can help cannabis businesses contribute positively to society, address historical injustices, and build a sustainable and equitable future for all stakeholders.

Engaging with the community

Engaging with the community is a critical aspect for businesses in the cannabis industry, particularly for medical marijuana dispensaries. This engagement not only fosters a positive relationship between the dispensary and the local community but also plays a significant role in normalizing cannabis, educating the public, and addressing historical injustices associated with cannabis prohibition. Effective community engagement involves a series of thoughtful, deliberate actions that demonstrate the dispensary's commitment to being a responsible and beneficial presence in the community.

At the heart of community engagement is the recognition of the dispensary as more than just a business; it is a healthcare provider, an educator, and a community partner. Dispensaries can initiate and participate in various activities that contribute positively to the community's well-being. For example, hosting educational seminars and workshops about the medical benefits of cannabis, safe consumption practices, and legal rights regarding medical marijuana use can help demystify cannabis and empower individuals with knowledge.

Participating in local events, such as health fairs, community festivals, and charity fundraisers, allows dispensaries to integrate themselves into the fabric of the community. These events provide opportunities to engage with community members, answer questions about cannabis, and demonstrate the dispensary's commitment to public health and wellness. Sponsorships of local sports teams, arts programs, or community initiatives can also enhance the dispensary's visibility and reputation as a community supporter.

Community service projects and charitable activities are another avenue for engagement. Dispensaries can organize or participate in food drives, park clean-ups, and other volunteer activities that address local needs. Collaborating with non-profit organizations, especially those focused on drug education, addiction recovery, or supporting populations disproportionately affected by cannabis prohibition, can amplify the dispensary's impact and contribute to social equity.

Engagement also means listening to and addressing community concerns. This can involve holding open forums or town hall meetings where community members can voice their opinions, ask questions, and learn more about the dispensary's operations, security measures, and contributions to the community. Transparency about business practices and responsiveness to feedback are crucial in building trust and mutual respect.

Advocacy and policy engagement represent another dimension of community involvement. Dispensaries can play a role in advocating for cannabis policy reform, including efforts to expunge cannabis-related criminal records, ensure equitable access to cannabis business licenses, and direct cannabis tax revenues to community development projects. By engaging in policy discussions and supporting reform initiatives, dispensaries can contribute to broader social change and justice.

To maximize the impact of community engagement efforts, dispensaries should communicate regularly about their activities through various channels, including social media, newsletters, and local media outlets. Sharing stories of community involvement, patient testimonials, and the positive outcomes of advocacy efforts can inspire others and encourage broader community support for the dispensary and the cannabis industry as a whole.

Engaging with the community is a multifaceted endeavor that requires dispensaries to act as educators, advocates, and responsible business operators. Through active participation in community life, dispensaries can build strong, positive relationships, contribute to public health and education, and play a role in shaping a more informed, equitable, and cannabis-friendly society.

Environmental Considerations

Environmental considerations in the cannabis industry are increasingly coming to the forefront as the sector expands rapidly. The cultivation, production, and distribution of cannabis have significant environmental impacts, including water usage, energy consumption, waste generation, and pesticide use. As awareness grows, both businesses and consumers are seeking ways to mitigate these impacts, making environmental sustainability a critical aspect of the cannabis industry's development.

Water usage is a major concern, particularly in regions prone to drought. Cannabis plants are water-intensive, requiring a steady supply throughout their growth cycle. Sustainable water management practices, such as rainwater harvesting, drip irrigation, and recirculating hydroponic systems, can significantly reduce water consumption and lessen the industry's impact on local water resources.

Energy consumption is another significant environmental consideration, especially in indoor cultivation operations. These facilities often rely on high-intensity lighting, climate control systems, and ventilation, leading to substantial electricity use. Transitioning to energy-efficient lighting options, like LED lights, implementing energy management systems, and utilizing renewable energy sources can reduce the carbon footprint of cannabis operations. Additionally, outdoor and greenhouse cultivation methods, which leverage natural light, can offer more sustainable alternatives to indoor cultivation, depending on the climate and regulatory environment.

Waste generation in the cannabis industry, from cultivation waste to packaging, poses environmental challenges. Cultivation operations produce organic waste, including plant trimmings and soil, which can be composted or repurposed rather than sent to landfills. Packaging waste, particularly single-use plastics prevalent in product packaging, is a growing concern. Efforts to reduce packaging waste include using recyclable or biodegradable materials, minimizing packaging size, and implementing take-back programs for used containers.

The use of pesticides and fertilizers in cannabis cultivation can have detrimental effects on soil health, water quality, and local ecosystems. Pesticide runoff can contaminate waterways, harming aquatic life and potentially impacting human health. Adopting organic cultivation practices, using natural pest management solutions, and selecting environmentally friendly fertilizers can mitigate these impacts and promote soil health and biodiversity.

Beyond operational practices, the cannabis industry can engage in broader environmental stewardship initiatives. This might include investing in conservation efforts, supporting reforestation projects, or participating in local environmental clean-up activities. Such initiatives demonstrate the industry's commitment to protecting and preserving the natural environment.

Environmental considerations are not just a matter of regulatory compliance or operational efficiency; they reflect the cannabis industry's responsibility to the planet and future generations. As the industry continues to evolve, integrating sustainability into every aspect of operations will be key to minimizing environmental impacts and ensuring the long-term viability of the cannabis sector. Adopting sustainable practices can also provide competitive advantages, appealing to environmentally conscious consumers and aligning with the values of a growing segment of the market.

Scaling and Expansion

Scaling and expansion in the cannabis industry require a strategic and comprehensive approach, given the unique challenges and opportunities this rapidly evolving market presents. As dispensaries and cannabis businesses look to grow, they must navigate regulatory landscapes, maintain product quality and consistency, manage supply chain complexities, and meet increasing customer expectations. Here's a closer look at key considerations for successfully scaling and expanding in the cannabis industry.

Understanding Regulatory Constraints

The regulatory environment is a critical factor in the cannabis industry, with laws and regulations varying significantly across different jurisdictions. Expansion plans must account for the legal frameworks governing cannabis in new markets, including licensing requirements, product testing and labeling standards, and restrictions on marketing and sales. A thorough understanding of these regulatory landscapes is essential for strategic planning and risk management.

Maintaining Product Quality and Consistency

As businesses scale, maintaining the quality and consistency of cannabis products becomes increasingly challenging. Standardizing cultivation and production processes, implementing rigorous quality control measures, and investing in staff training are essential to ensure that product quality remains high as operations expand. Consistency in product offerings builds trust with customers and is crucial for establishing a strong brand reputation.

Supply Chain Management

Scaling operations often involves expanding the supply chain, which can introduce complexities in sourcing, logistics, and inventory management. Building strong relationships with reliable suppliers, diversifying sourcing options, and leveraging technology for supply chain optimization can help manage these challenges. Effective inventory management strategies, such as demand forecasting and just-in-time inventory practices, are also critical for balancing product availability with storage and capital constraints.

Financial Planning and Access to Capital

Expansion requires significant investment, making robust financial planning and access to capital key components of scaling strategies. This may involve securing financing through loans, attracting investors, or reinvesting profits. Understanding the unique financial challenges of the cannabis industry, including banking restrictions and tax implications, is crucial for effective financial management and fundraising.

Investing in Technology and Automation

Technology plays a pivotal role in scaling cannabis businesses, from cultivation and production to sales and customer engagement. Automation technologies can improve efficiency in operations, reduce labor costs, and enhance product consistency. Investing in business management software, including POS systems, inventory management platforms, and customer relationship management (CRM) tools, can streamline operations and support growth.

Market Research and Customer Engagement

Understanding market trends, customer preferences, and competitive landscapes is essential for successful expansion. Market research can inform product development, marketing strategies, and service offerings, tailoring them to meet the needs of new customer segments. Engaging with customers through marketing, community involvement, and personalized service helps build brand loyalty and supports market penetration.

Strategic Partnerships and Collaborations

Forming strategic partnerships and collaborations can provide valuable opportunities for scaling and expansion. This might include partnerships with other cannabis businesses, cross-industry collaborations, or alliances with research institutions. Such partnerships can expand market reach, enhance product offerings, and contribute to innovation.

Adapting to Market Changes

The cannabis industry is characterized by rapid change, with evolving regulations, shifting consumer preferences, and emerging market opportunities. Businesses must remain adaptable, continuously assessing their strategies and operations and being prepared to pivot in response to market changes.

Scaling and expansion in the cannabis industry require careful planning, adaptability, and a deep understanding of the market and regulatory environment. By focusing on quality, efficiency, customer engagement, and strategic growth initiatives, cannabis businesses can navigate the complexities of expansion and capitalize on the opportunities in this dynamic industry.

Evaluating the Performance Of Your Dispensary

Evaluating the performance of your medical marijuana dispensary is a multifaceted process that involves analyzing various aspects of the business to ensure it meets its goals, satisfies patient needs, and operates within regulatory compliance. Performance evaluation is crucial not only for identifying areas of success but also for pinpointing opportunities for improvement, adapting to market changes, and making informed decisions that drive growth and sustainability.

At the core of performance evaluation is financial analysis, which provides a clear picture of the dispensary's profitability and financial health. This involves reviewing revenue streams, cost of goods sold (COGS), operating expenses, and net profit margins. Key financial ratios and metrics, such as return on investment (ROI), inventory turnover rates, and gross margin return on investment (GMROI), can offer insights into the efficiency and effectiveness of the dispensary's operations. Comparing these financial indicators against industry benchmarks and historical performance data helps in assessing financial performance and identifying trends or issues that may require attention.

Beyond financial metrics, evaluating customer satisfaction is vital for understanding how well the dispensary meets patient needs and expectations. Patient feedback, whether collected through surveys, online reviews, or direct interactions, provides valuable insights into the quality of service, product offerings, and overall patient experience. Analyzing this feedback can highlight strengths in customer service as well as areas for improvement, informing strategies to enhance patient satisfaction and loyalty.

Inventory management efficiency is another critical aspect of performance evaluation. Effective inventory management ensures that the dispensary maintains an optimal balance of products to meet patient demand without overstocking or understocking. Key indicators of inventory management performance include product sell-through rates, days on hand, and stockouts or overstock incidents. Regularly reviewing these metrics can help optimize inventory levels, reduce waste, and improve product availability.

Regulatory compliance is a non-negotiable aspect of operating a medical marijuana dispensary, making compliance monitoring an essential part of performance evaluation. This includes ensuring that all operations adhere to state and local cannabis regulations, from product testing and labeling to security measures and patient verification processes. Regular audits and compliance checks can help identify and address any potential regulatory issues, reducing the risk of fines, penalties, or license revocation.

Employee performance and engagement also play a significant role in the overall success of the dispensary. Assessing staff knowledge, customer service skills, and operational efficiency can identify training needs and opportunities to improve team performance. Employee satisfaction surveys and feedback mechanisms can gauge staff engagement and morale, which are critical for retaining a motivated and high-performing team.

Evaluating the dispensary's market position and competitive performance is crucial for strategic planning. This involves analyzing market trends, patient demographics, and competitive dynamics to assess the dispensary's market share, brand recognition, and competitive advantages. Understanding the dispensary's position in the market can inform marketing strategies, product offerings, and business development initiatives to enhance competitive performance and drive growth.

Opportunities for Scaling and Expansion

Opportunities for scaling and expansion in the medical marijuana industry are vast, reflecting the sector's rapid growth and evolving regulatory landscape. As more states and countries legalize medical cannabis, dispensaries and related businesses are exploring innovative ways to grow their operations, reach new patient demographics, and diversify their product offerings. Key opportunities for scaling and expansion include geographic expansion, product line diversification, vertical integration, embracing technology, and strategic partnerships.

Geographic expansion is a primary avenue for growth, allowing dispensaries to enter new markets where medical cannabis has been legalized. This requires a deep understanding of the regulatory environment in new jurisdictions, as well as market research to understand patient needs and competitive landscapes. Establishing new storefronts in different locations can increase a dispensary's patient base and brand presence. However, success in geographic expansion depends on careful planning, compliance with local regulations, and the ability to adapt operations and product offerings to meet local preferences.

Product line diversification offers another opportunity for growth. By expanding their range of products, dispensaries can cater to a broader spectrum of patient needs and preferences. This might include introducing new cannabis strains, edibles, topicals, concentrates, and CBD products. Product innovation, driven by patient feedback and market trends, can differentiate a dispensary in a competitive market. Additionally, offering ancillary products related to cannabis use, such as vaporizers and accessories, can provide new revenue streams.

Vertical integration represents a strategic approach to scaling, allowing dispensaries to control the entire supply chain from cultivation to retail. By growing their cannabis or manufacturing their products, dispensaries can ensure product quality, reduce costs, and improve supply chain reliability. Vertical integration requires significant investment and expertise in cultivation and production but can offer greater control over product availability, pricing, and brand consistency.

Embracing technology is critical for scaling operations efficiently. Advanced point-of-sale (POS) systems, inventory management software, and customer relationship management (CRM) platforms can streamline operations, enhance patient engagement, and provide valuable data insights for decision-making. E-commerce platforms and online ordering options can expand a dispensary's reach, offering convenience to patients and capturing a larger market share. Investing in digital marketing and social media can also raise brand awareness and attract new patients.

Strategic partnerships and collaborations can facilitate growth and expansion in the medical marijuana industry. Forming alliances with healthcare providers, research institutions, and advocacy groups can enhance a dispensary's credibility and patient referrals. Collaborating with other cannabis businesses for cross-promotion or co-branding initiatives can broaden market exposure. Partnerships with technology providers can lead to innovative solutions that improve patient care and operational efficiency.

The medical marijuana industry presents numerous opportunities for scaling and expansion, driven by ongoing legalization efforts, patient demand, and technological advancements. Whether through geographic expansion, product diversification, vertical integration, technological innovation, or strategic partnerships, dispensaries can explore various pathways to growth. Success in scaling and expansion requires careful strategic planning, a deep understanding of regulatory and market dynamics, and a commitment to quality patient care and product excellence.

Strategies for Growth and Diversification

Strategies for growth and diversification in the medical marijuana industry are essential for businesses looking to capitalize on the expanding market and navigate the complex regulatory landscape. As the industry matures, dispensaries and cannabis companies must explore innovative ways to grow their operations, reach new customers, and mitigate risks associated with market fluctuations and regulatory changes.

Here's an in-depth exploration of effective strategies for growth and diversification.

Geographic Expansion

One of the primary strategies for growth is geographic expansion. By entering new markets where medical cannabis has been legalized, dispensaries can tap into new customer bases and increase their market share. This strategy requires thorough research to understand the regulatory requirements, competitive landscape, and patient needs in the new location. Successful geographic expansion often involves tailoring product offerings and marketing strategies to fit local preferences and cultural nuances.

Product Line Diversification

Diversifying the product lineup allows dispensaries to cater to a broader range of patient preferences and medical needs. This can include introducing new cannabis strains, edibles, concentrates, topicals, and CBD products. Beyond cannabis products, dispensaries can also diversify into wellness products and services that complement medical marijuana use, such as acupuncture, massage, or yoga classes. Product diversification not only attracts new customers but also enhances the shopping experience for existing patients.

Investing in Technology

Technology plays a crucial role in scaling and diversification efforts. Implementing advanced point-of-sale (POS) systems, inventory management software, and customer relationship management (CRM) platforms can streamline operations and enhance patient engagement. E-commerce and mobile applications offer convenient shopping options for patients, expanding the dispensary's reach beyond its physical location. Investing in data analytics tools can also provide valuable insights into customer behavior, product trends, and operational efficiency, informing strategic decisions.

Vertical Integration

Vertical integration involves controlling multiple stages of the supply chain, from cultivation to retail. For dispensaries, vertical integration can offer several advantages, including cost savings, improved supply chain control, and product quality assurance. By growing their cannabis or manufacturing their products, dispensaries can differentiate their brand and ensure a consistent supply of high-quality products. However, vertical integration requires significant investment and operational expertise in cultivation and production.

Strategic Partnerships and Collaborations

Forming strategic partnerships and collaborations can facilitate growth and diversification. This might include partnering with healthcare providers to increase patient referrals, collaborating with research institutions on cannabis studies, or co-branding products with other cannabis companies. Partnerships with non-cannabis businesses can also open up new markets and distribution channels. Through collaboration, dispensaries can leverage complementary strengths and resources to achieve mutual growth objectives.

Focus on Branding and Marketing

Strong branding and marketing are essential for standing out in the competitive cannabis market. Developing a distinct brand identity that resonates with your target audience can foster customer loyalty and attract new patients. Effective marketing strategies, including digital marketing, social media, and community engagement, can raise brand awareness and communicate the dispensary's value proposition. Content marketing that educates patients about cannabis and its medical benefits can also position the dispensary as a trusted authority in the field.

Regulatory Compliance and Advocacy

Navigating the regulatory landscape is a constant challenge in the cannabis industry. Ensuring compliance with state and local regulations is critical for operational continuity and reputation. Additionally, engaging in advocacy efforts for favorable cannabis policies can contribute to a more stable and growth-friendly regulatory environment. Active participation in industry associations and policy discussions can also enhance the dispensary's visibility and influence in the cannabis community.

Implementing strategies for growth and diversification requires a balance of innovation, risk management, and strategic planning. By exploring new markets, diversifying product offerings, leveraging technology, forming strategic partnerships, and focusing on strong branding and regulatory compliance, dispensaries and cannabis companies can achieve sustainable growth and success in the evolving medical marijuana industry.

Legal and Industry Updates

Keeping abreast of legal and industry updates in the cannabis sector is crucial for businesses operating within this space. The legal landscape surrounding cannabis is in a constant state of flux, with regulations evolving at both the state and federal levels. Similarly, industry trends, consumer preferences, and technological advancements can shift rapidly, influencing business operations, product development, and marketing strategies.

Here's a closer look at why staying updated is essential and how businesses can effectively monitor these changes.

Why Staying Updated is Critical

1. Regulatory Compliance: Legal updates often involve changes to licensing requirements, product testing standards, packaging and labeling rules, and sales regulations. Staying informed ensures that businesses remain compliant, avoiding fines, legal penalties, or the revocation of operating licenses.

2. Market Adaptation: Industry updates provide insights into emerging trends, consumer behavior, and competitive dynamics. Businesses that are quick to adapt can capitalize on new

opportunities, differentiate themselves from competitors, and meet changing consumer demands more effectively.

3. Risk Management: Understanding the legal and regulatory environment helps businesses anticipate and mitigate risks associated with policy changes. This is particularly important for financial planning, investment decisions, and strategic growth initiatives.

4. Advocacy and Influence: Being informed about legislative developments enables businesses to participate in advocacy efforts and influence policy making. Active engagement in policy discussions can contribute to shaping a favorable regulatory framework for the cannabis industry.

Strategies for Staying Updated

1. Regulatory Alerts and Newsletters: Subscribing to regulatory alerts and newsletters from state cannabis control boards, industry associations, and legal firms specializing in cannabis law can provide timely updates on legal changes. These resources often offer expert analyses and interpretations of new regulations and their implications for businesses.

2. Industry Conferences and Trade Shows: Attending industry conferences, trade shows, and webinars is an effective way to stay informed about market trends, innovations, and regulatory issues.

These events also offer networking opportunities with other professionals who can share insights and experiences.

3. Professional Networks and Forums: Joining professional networks and online forums dedicated to the cannabis industry can facilitate information exchange and discussions about legal changes, industry trends, and best practices. Peer insights can provide practical perspectives on navigating challenges and seizing opportunities.

4. Consulting Legal and Industry Experts: Establishing relationships with legal experts and industry consultants can provide businesses with tailored advice and updates relevant to their operations. These professionals can help interpret complex regulations and guide strategic decision-making.

5. Continuous Education: Participating in continuous education programs, workshops, and courses on cannabis law, business management, and industry-specific topics can enhance a business's ability to adapt to changes. Many educational institutions and industry organizations offer programs designed to keep cannabis professionals at the forefront of the field.

6. Monitoring Research and Publications: Keeping an eye on academic research, industry reports, and publications can offer insights into consumer trends, technological advancements, and

potential regulatory shifts. This information can inform product development, marketing strategies, and operational improvements.

Staying informed about legal and industry updates is essential for navigating the complexities of the cannabis sector. By leveraging a variety of resources and strategies to monitor changes, businesses can ensure regulatory compliance, adapt to market dynamics, manage risks effectively, and actively participate in shaping the industry's future.

Staying informed about legal changes

Staying informed about legal changes in the cannabis industry is crucial for businesses to remain compliant and competitive. The regulatory landscape for cannabis is dynamic, with frequent updates to laws and regulations at the state, federal, and international levels. These changes can impact various aspects of the cannabis business, including licensing, product testing, packaging, advertising, and sales practices.

Here's a comprehensive approach to keeping abreast of legal changes in the cannabis industry.

Subscribing to Regulatory Updates

Many government agencies and regulatory bodies offer subscription services for updates on laws and regulations. By subscribing to these alerts, businesses can receive timely notifications about proposed changes, new regulations, and compliance deadlines directly from the source. This service is often available on the websites of state cannabis control boards, health departments, and federal agencies.

Engaging with Industry Associations

Industry associations play a critical role in monitoring legal changes, advocating for the industry, and providing resources to their members. Membership in these associations can offer access to legal updates, educational resources, and expert analyses of how new regulations may affect businesses. These associations frequently communicate updates through newsletters, webinars, and conferences.

Utilizing Legal and Compliance Services

Specialized legal and compliance firms that focus on the cannabis industry can be invaluable resources for staying informed about legal changes. These firms monitor regulatory developments closely and provide guidance on compliance strategies. Engaging their services or subscribing to their updates can help businesses navigate the complexities of cannabis regulations.

Attending Conferences and Seminars

Conferences, seminars, and workshops focused on the cannabis industry often feature sessions on legal and regulatory issues. These events provide opportunities to learn from legal experts, regulators, and industry leaders about recent changes and emerging legal trends. They also offer a platform for networking and sharing experiences with peers who may have faced similar compliance challenges.

Participating in Advocacy and Policy Groups

Being active in advocacy and policy groups can provide insights into legislative trends and regulatory changes. These groups work to influence cannabis policy and can offer members advanced notice of potential legal shifts. Participation can also provide businesses with a voice in the regulatory process, allowing them to advocate for fair and sensible cannabis laws.

Monitoring Legal Publications and News Outlets

Numerous legal publications and news outlets cover the cannabis industry, providing updates on legal changes, court rulings, and regulatory trends. Regularly reading these publications can help businesses stay informed about the legal landscape. Many offer email newsletters or alert services to deliver the latest news directly to subscribers.

Creating a Compliance Calendar

A compliance calendar can help businesses track important regulatory deadlines, such as license renewals, reporting requirements, and compliance certification dates. This tool ensures that key legal obligations are not overlooked and can aid in planning for regulatory changes.

Continuous Training and Education

Ongoing training and education for staff on regulatory compliance are essential. This can include formal training programs, regular compliance meetings, and updates on legal changes. Educating employees about the legal responsibilities of the business and their role in maintaining compliance is critical for preventing violations.

Staying informed about legal changes in the cannabis industry requires a multifaceted approach, including leveraging government resources, engaging with industry associations, consulting with legal experts, participating in educational events, and implementing internal processes for compliance management. By staying informed and proactive, cannabis businesses can navigate the evolving regulatory landscape successfully.

Keeping Up With Industry Trends

Keeping up with industry trends in the rapidly evolving cannabis market is essential for businesses looking to stay competitive and meet the changing needs and preferences of consumers. The cannabis industry is characterized by swift advancements in cultivation techniques, product innovation, regulatory changes, and shifts in consumer behavior. Staying informed about these trends can help businesses anticipate market shifts, adapt their strategies, and seize new opportunities.

Here's how businesses can keep up with industry trends effectively:

Participate in Trade Shows and Conferences

Attending trade shows, conferences, and expos dedicated to the cannabis industry is one of the most direct ways to stay abreast of new trends, technologies, and products. These events offer valuable opportunities to network with other professionals, learn from industry leaders, and discover emerging trends in real-time. Additionally, participating in panel discussions, workshops, and seminars can provide deeper insights into specific areas of interest.

Leverage Industry Reports and Market Research

Numerous market research firms and industry analysts publish reports and studies that offer comprehensive insights into market trends, consumer preferences, and future industry projections. Subscribing to these reports or accessing summaries can help businesses understand the broader market landscape, identify growth opportunities, and make data-driven decisions.

Engage with Online Communities and Social Media

Online forums, social media platforms, and professional networks are rich sources of real-time information and discussions about the cannabis industry. Following influencers, thought leaders, and industry-specific groups on platforms like LinkedIn, Twitter, and Instagram can provide quick updates on emerging trends, industry news, and consumer sentiment. Participating in discussions and engaging with content can also foster connections with other industry professionals.

Subscribe to Industry Publications

There are many reputable cannabis industry publications, both online and in print, that cover the latest news, research, and developments in the field. Regularly reading these publications can keep you informed about regulatory changes, technological advancements, and business strategies within the cannabis sector.

Many offer newsletters or alert services to deliver the latest content directly to your inbox.

Monitor Consumer Feedback and Reviews

Consumer feedback, whether through direct interactions, online reviews, or social media comments, can provide early indicators of shifting preferences and emerging trends. Paying attention to what consumers are saying about products, brands, and their overall experiences can help businesses tailor their offerings to meet evolving demands.

Collaborate with Research Institutions and Universities

Some research institutions and universities conduct cutting-edge studies on cannabis, including its medical applications, consumer usage patterns, and impact on society. Collaborating with these institutions or staying informed about their research findings can offer unique insights into future trends and scientific advancements in the cannabis industry.

Implement a Continuous Learning Culture

Fostering a culture of continuous learning within your organization encourages employees at all levels to seek out and share knowledge about industry trends and innovations. This can include organizing regular training sessions, encouraging attendance at industry events, and providing access to educational resources. A well-informed team can be a valuable asset in identifying and responding to new trends.

Conclusion

Keeping up with industry trends in the rapidly evolving cannabis sector is crucial for businesses aiming to stay competitive and responsive to market demands. The landscape of the cannabis industry is characterized by swift changes in legal regulations, consumer preferences, technological advancements, and innovative product developments. As such, businesses that are proactive in monitoring and adapting to these trends can seize new opportunities, navigate challenges more effectively, and position themselves for sustained growth and success.

The importance of staying informed about legal changes cannot be overstated, given the complex regulatory environment surrounding cannabis. Businesses must navigate these regulations meticulously to ensure compliance, avoid penalties, and capitalize on new market opportunities as they arise. Engaging with legal experts, subscribing to regulatory updates, and participating in industry associations are effective strategies for staying abreast of legal developments.

Understanding and responding to consumer trends is essential for meeting patient and consumer needs. This involves not just tracking changes in consumer preferences but also anticipating future demand for products and services. Investing in market research, engaging with customers directly, and monitoring social media and online forums can provide valuable insights into consumer behavior and preferences.

Technological advancements are transforming the cannabis industry, from cultivation and production processes to retail and customer engagement strategies. Embracing these technologies can enhance operational efficiency, improve product quality, and create more personalized and engaging customer experiences. Businesses should stay informed about technological trends and evaluate how these innovations can be integrated into their operations.

The cannabis industry's growth is fostering a competitive landscape, making differentiation more important than ever. Businesses can stand out by focusing on quality, sustainability, and community engagement, aligning their operations with broader social and environmental values. This approach not only appeals to a growing segment of conscious consumers but also contributes to the industry's positive social impact.

In conclusion, keeping up with industry trends in the cannabis sector is a dynamic and ongoing process that requires vigilance, flexibility, and a forward-looking approach. By staying informed about legal developments, consumer preferences, technological advancements, and competitive dynamics, cannabis businesses can navigate the complexities of the market, meet the evolving needs of their customers, and achieve long-term success in this exciting and challenging industry.

www.ingramcontent.com/pod-product-compliance
Lightning Source LLC
Chambersburg PA
CBHW071914210526
45479CB00002B/421